MORE
LONDON
PIANO MAKERS

Front cover illustration:
Love at First Sight: the Eavestaff minipiano finds a home
[From a W.G. Eavestaff & Sons publicity brochure, circa 1940. Author's collection]

Rear cover:
Herbert Lowrey's model 109 Rogers upright, 1968
[From a Rogers promotional brochure. Author's collection]

MORE LONDON PIANO MAKERS

EAVESTAFF
ROGERS • SQUIRE • KNIGHT
CHAPPELL • HOPKINSON

A sequel to *Five London Piano Makers:*
Brinsmead, Challen, Collard,
Danemann & Welmar
(2010)

ALASTAIR LAURENCE

Published by the author

in association with

Keyword Press
291 Sprowston Mews
London E7 9AE
England

KEYWORD PRESS

www.keywordpress.co.uk

© Dr. Alastair Laurence 2015

First published 2015

ISBN 978-0-9555590-4-4

All rights reserved

Except as provided for by statute, no part of this book may be reproduced or converted into electronic form without the prior written permission of Keyword Press

The right of Alastair Laurence to be identified as the author of this work has been asserted in accordance with the Copyright, Designs and Patents Act 1988

British Library Cataloguing in Publication Data

A catalogue record for this book is available from the British Library

Printed by
Pioneer Press Limited
Skipton
North Yorkshire
BD23 2TZ

CONTENTS

Acknowledgements	Page	vii
Introduction		ix
1. The Chappell Piano Company		1
2. Eavestaff, Brasted Brothers and the *Minipiano*		19
3. The Squire family of Piano Makers		39
4. Rogers and Hopkinson		57
5. Alfred Knight		80
Notes		103
Appendix 1	A list of employees of the Chappell Piano Company who lost their lives in World War I	115
Appendix 2	A Chappell Retail Price List, October 1929, and a Rogers Retail Price List, c. 1938	116
Appendix 3	An outline tree of the Brasted family of pianomakers	118
Appendix 4	A checklist of new models of upright, grand and minipianos introduced by Brasted Brothers Ltd between 1930 and 1969	119
Appendix 5	An outline tree of the Squire family of piano makers	120
Appendix 6	The last will of William Brinsmead Squire, made 15th March 1862, proved 8th March 1864	121
Appendix 7	An outline tree of the Hopkinson family of piano makers	123
Appendix 8	A selection of favourable testimonials which had been received by the firm of George Rogers & Sons by circa 1933	124
Appendix 9	The reminiscences of George Veness, who was working at the Rogers/Hopkinson factory during the early 1970s	126
Appendix 10	Key Knight personnel involved in piano manufacture, c.1950 - 1990	128
Appendix 11	Lowest retail prices for various English upright models, May 1969	129

ACKNOWLEDGEMENTS

THE author wishes to express his gratitude for the valuable information, or advice, or illustrative material, received from the following:

Marcus Bath, Heinz Bossenroth; Robert Brasted; the staff of the British Library, Colindale Avenue, London NW9 5HE; Heritage Image Partnership Ltd., London; Steven Hermitage; the staff of Essex County Record Office, Chelmsford CM2 6YT; Ferguson Hoey; John Hopkinson; Charles & Caroline Hopkinson; Jean Jamieson, archivist, Falkirk Council, Callendar Park, Falkirk FK1 1YR; Bill & Beth Kibby of the Piano History Centre, Great Yarmouth NR31 0JB; Allan Lanstein; Andrew Levine; Laura Little; Joseph Marsh; Mary and James McLauchlan; David Pescod; Pierce Piano Atlas; David Short; Frank Squire; David Thomas; George Veness; Michael Vivian; Helen Weedon; Steven Woodward; Allen Wright; Sylvia & Michael York; and the late Patrick Booth, Percy Cossins, Charles Gilbey, A. L. Hodgson and Sydney Paradine.

In particular, the author also wishes to express his appreciation to Marie Kent, for the many hours she has spent in making searches on the author's behalf at Colindale Periodicals Library, Hendon, and also for her assistance in the checking of the final drafts and proofs for this book. Last but not least, the author wishes to extend his thanks to Peter Bavington of *Keyword Press*, the general editor and distributor of *More London Piano Makers*. Peter has also scrutinised the drafts and proofs of this book; he has made many helpful comments and suggestions along the way, and given valued support generally.

INTRODUCTION

IN January 2010, the author of this book offered the piano-loving public his publication, *Five London Piano Makers*, which features the histories of five well-known makes of piano: Brinsmead, Challen, Collard, Danemann and Welmar. By a happy coincidence, the choice of these five firms represented a very good 'cross section' within the piano-making industry, ranging from Collard, a company with antique roots extending back over two hundred years into the eighteenth century, to Welmar and Danemann, which were essentially twentieth-century enterprises.

All five firms made *good* pianos, and all of them had the distinction of producing large concert grand models for recitals in public halls – which means that each can be considered to have made a worthy contribution to the musical culture of the nation. This contribution also extended globally, to concert halls in far-flung parts of the former British Empire, where London-built concert grands were once supplied. In spite of the achievements of each of the five, however, there was a genuine fear that important surviving information concerning them was in danger of disappearing for ever – and within a matter of a few years; and so the author felt compelled to get something down in writing, in order to at least preserve a kind of 'record'.

Since 2010, the author has been repeatedly asked whether there will be a sequel to his book. This possibility was hinted at in the introduction to *Five London Piano Makers*. There is now, at last, sufficient material assembled to offer this sequel. *More London Piano Makers* contains five chapters dealing with five other (but equally interesting) firms, groups of companies, or piano-making families. This time, the chosen five are: Chappell; Eavestaff/

Brasted; Squire; Rogers/Hopkinson; and Knight. Like the earlier *Five London Piano Makers*, this new volume is also peppered with a wide variety of illustrations, and eleven useful appendices appear at the end of the main account.

The Chappell Piano Company, which is featured in chapter 1, made some of the finest grand or upright pianos ever seen in this country; and yet the activities of the Company and its products have been sadly neglected or forgotten by writers on music in recent years. The Chappell piano, particularly the magnificent concert grand designed by the legendary Reinhold Glandt, appears to have become slowly and sadly lost from musicians' memories. Few individuals today will be aware that Chappell concert grands were once a regular feature on the platforms of the Royal Albert Hall and the former Queen's Hall, London. As a mere 'trade', rather than a profession, the making of Chappell instruments was long relegated to the extreme sidelines of the London cultural and musical world. The glamour of the firm's West End headquarters at 50, New Bond Street, with its close personal associations with famous musicians and composers, contrasted strongly with the shabby and largely neglected Chappell manufactory in Camden Town. We can even suggest that the historical importance of the Chappell piano was never grasped by the later proprietors of the Chappell publishing company itself, when we observe how they continued to manufacture instruments in such a half-hearted, aimless way in the years prior to the factory's closure in 1970.

The second chapter in this book looks at a commercial curiosity which as a musical instrument and an item of furniture contrasts strongly in almost every way with pianos produced by Chappell: this is the 'minipiano', manufactured by Brasted Brothers Ltd, with the brand name *Eavestaff* attached. Whilst Chappell produced the largest and most expensive grands made in London, Brasted Brothers' minipianos for a number of years appear to have been the smallest and cheapest kind of piano available for anyone to purchase. With its extraordinary diminutive size but clear and sweet tonal quality, the minipiano certainly enjoyed something of a vogue from the mid-to-late 1930s until the mid 1950s. To acquire one, in whichever choice of casework design or polish, was to be at the forefront of fashion. Brasted Brothers were ambitiously determined to become the largest volume producer of pianos in Britain, and they appear to have achieved this by the year 1936. Their piano manufactory at Harringay, north London, was long considered to be the largest of its kind in Europe. By turning out vast quantities of minipianos and other kinds of upright or grand instruments, the price of each model was kept down, and so a piano of some sorts became affordable by many a family for the first time.

In chapter three, we turn to something of a phenomenon: the involvement of an army of Squires in the piano industry. We can count up to twenty-two related individuals, but there were probably more. The family was active in piano making, tuning or retailing from the late 1820s until the 1970s. Members of the piano-tuning profession have long puzzled over the wide range of variant 'Squire' pianos they meet in the course of their work, whether pianos bearing the names, for example, of *B. Squire & Son, Henry Squire, William Squire* or even *Squire & Longson*. This chapter gives them the chance, at last, to sort out who from whom. The Squire family comprised a curious spectrum of individuals, some endearing, some eccentric, and all of them with a high level of manual skill, but – as an unfortunate recurring family trait – often reckless with money. William and Betsy Squire's decision to create a children's playground on the roof of their factory for their ten offspring is one of the entertaining stories which appears in this book! Frank Squire's practice of striking his employees' handiwork with a small silver hammer as a mark of disapproval is certainly less endearing; nevertheless, we admire Frank's remarkable resilience and tenacity in surviving as a manufacturer until his eighty-seventh year.

In chapter four, we focus on the activities of two associated companies, who, like Chappell, made quality pianos: they are J. & J. Hopkinson and George Rogers & Sons. Their tie-up can be precisely dated from March 1924, when the ailing Hopkinson firm was purchased by Dr Charles Vincent's Rogers company. Of the two firms, Hopkinson traces its origins back to Leeds, Yorkshire, where its founding partners, the brothers John and James Hopkinson, lived and worked. By the year 1846 they had moved their business to London; by 1866 they were employing over one hundred craftsmen and apprentices at their new Fitzroy Road factory, Primrose Hill. The second half of the nineteenth century was perhaps the Hopkinson's heyday: the firm's instruments were highly regarded for their tonal qualities, and, in common with Broadwood, Collard, Chappell, Challen and Brinsmead, the Hopkinson business ranked among the largest of the London makers. In 1907, the company was joined by a new factory manager, Frank Challen, who created an outstanding range of new models which further enhanced the firm's reputation; but in the years following the First World War, the company was financially mismanaged, and it went into receivership in 1924.

George Rogers & Sons, from the date of that company's founding in 1843, was a considerably smaller enterprise than Hopkinson, with its roots in the centre of Camden Town. For many years it was run by the brothers Tom and Charles Rogers, who employed the talents of Samuel Wolfenden to design a range of new models which came to be regarded as the 'English Bechstein' on account of their excellent musical qualities. Then, around the year 1913, the Rogers firm was acquired by Dr Charles Vincent, an organist who also happened to have a considerable level of financial clout at his fingertips. As we have seen, in March 1924 he was able to purchase J. & J. Hopkinson; and thereafter from that date until 2003, the two brand names – Rogers and Hopkinson – continued to be placed on identical London-made instruments.

The last chapter of this book dwells on the career of the remarkable Alfred Knight, who not only designed his own pianos, supervised their manufacture, and successfully marketed them, but, in addition, could play them extremely well. He was some kind of a genius, and his warm, affable personality (which obviously helped to sell his pianos!) has been long-remembered in the piano trade. During the 1920s, Knight was lucky to have worked in a managerial capacity with the firm of Cremona Ltd, makers of the *Squire & Longson* piano. There, he experimented with new designs of instrument, and the experience gained from this was of great benefit to him when he eventually established his own enterprises some years later. The first of these, Booker & Knight (1931) was set up to manufacture the *Marshall & Rose* piano. From 1936, his second company, Alfred Knight Ltd, began to turn out the K6, K10 and K15, small upright models which were to become world famous. After 1945, Knight ambitiously established manufacturing plants in Oslo and Johannesburg, where his pianos could be assembled using components made in England. For his achievements in the world of music and in the field of exports, Alfred Knight was awarded an OBE in 1966.

All of the firms accounted for in *More London Piano Makers* no longer manufacture. The various Squire enterprises appear to have ceased trading long before the Second World War; both Chappell's and Brasted's factories closed down during 1970; the last independent factory making Rogers and Hopkinson instruments shut its doors in the early 1980s; and finally, Knight's own factory at Loughton was wound up in 1990. Since then, we have witnessed the slow but sure disintegration of piano-making skills in this country. The training of craftsmanship, the key element necessary for the survival of any piano making on these shores, has long been woefully inadequate and greatly undervalued. There are hardly any places left where the skills can be taught; and yet for many of a younger generation, the glamour of the virtual world seen on their computer screens, and the obsessive stroking of touch screens, rather than the more complex manual work of crafting musical instruments at the workbench, seems to give them satisfaction enough.

This indeed is a very dangerous situation – dangerous because we may reach a point where there is no one left to teach piano-making skills and to pass on critical knowledge to a new generation. The situation in this country contrasts with that in Germany and Japan, where manual skills seem to be more valued and respected in society, and where proper training is often readily available. It is not unrealistic to suggest that, in the years ahead, we may have to commission tuner technicians to fly in from Germany or Japan, just to keep our own pianos in reasonable order!

One of the purposes of this book is to show that London did, at one time, have a vigorous and flourishing piano industry, full of stimulating challenges, new ventures, and a great deal of 'job interest'. The centre of piano making was Camden Town, north London, where the various workshops, including some of those mentioned in this book, congregated. At the hub of this centre was the *Mother Redcap* public house (now called the *World's End*) opposite Camden Town tube station, which was a nerve centre of the whole industry, and which functioned as some kind of informal labour exchange. Hundreds of piano makers must have passed through its doors.

Employment in the piano trade in and around Camden Town in the period from 1860 to 1930 must have been a fascinating and highly memorable experience for many. The trade was full of colourful and entertaining 'personalities'; family 'dynasties' were prevalent; the streets were crowded with pianos or piano parts being trundled on hand-pushed barrows from one workshop to another; there was constant trade 'gossip' and intrigue; there was great pride in workmanship; there was a high level of interest as the features and qualities of one maker's pianos were carefully compared with another's; and of course, there was money to be made. It is the writer's hope that this book will arouse in the reader a feeling of nostalgia for that unique 'atmosphere' which characterised piano making in the London of a former age.

The writer also hopes that this book will remind the reader that, with the passing of almost every part of our nation's piano-making industry, we have lost something of a national treasure.

Whitby, North Yorkshire.

January 2015

*The magnificent cast-iron frame of the Chappell concert grand.
Designed by R.F. Glandt, c.1895.*
[Booth & Brookes ironfoundry archives, Essex County Record Office, Chelmsford]

1
THE CHAPPELL PIANO COMPANY

IN the field of music publishing, the name 'Chappell' is a household word. The publishing house's famous long-time headquarters at 50, New Bond Street in London's West End, would have been one of the most frequently visited of all the music stores in the capital, and one where an assortment of Chappell pianos would have been a regular feature on the showroom floor. In the upper floor rooms at the same address was to be found a treasure-trove: a vast collection of company archives and ephemera. Tragically, all the firm's records perished in a disastrous fire at New Bond Street in 1964, which gutted the building. Although number 50 was soon completely rebuilt, its historical contents were lost for ever.

With such an important primary source missing, how was a detailed or accurate account of the Chappell piano ever to be written? In order to assemble sufficient material for this chapter, recourse had to be made to alternative sources: first of all, elderly former Chappell employees from the Chalk Farm factory were interviewed and asked to recall their memories of manufacturing; then descendants of leading members of the Company were pestered for relevant material; visits to the old factory buildings in Chalk Farm were undertaken, to try and work out how the layout of the complex evolved; many editions of a monthly Trade journal, *The Pianomaker*, were pored over from cover to cover in order to try and find important, publicised events in the firm's history;[1] and last but not least, a number of Chappell instruments themselves were studied, in an attempt to gain the fullest appreciation of their qualities.

In spite of the fact that piano manufacturing was always regarded as very much a 'side line' of the great publishing house, we can assert the following: if we are ever obliged to name only *one* make of piano as being the 'best ever' made in Britain, then the Chappell has a strong claim to that honour. The firm's instruments seem to have had the edge on most other British manufactures. The Broadwood is probably the only other make in the same league, with some of the other quality firms such as Rogers, Hopkinson, Brinsmead, Collard, and Marshall & Rose following on closely behind in a list of contenders. What marks out the Chappell piano is this: from the late 1890s, the company went out of its way to manufacture a range of large grands of great tonal distinction, which soon became the first choice of many concert halls and music institutions throughout the land. Chappell, with Broadwood, was the only London maker during the opening decades of the twentieth century which was seriously tied up with the regular provision of concert grands for professional recital use.

Origins

Some writers tell us that the music-publishing house of Chappell was established in the year 1810; others suggest 1811; and yet others, 1812. A booklet to commemorate the supposed one hundred and fiftieth anniversary of the firm, entitled *The Chappell Story*, and compiled by Carlene Mair, was published in 1961; but out of its eighty-nine pages, only three of them are devoted to an account of the Chappell piano – and in a very superficial, glossed-over sort of way. The Chappell piano certainly deserved better, especially when one considers the tremendous reputation the instruments had in 1961.

For all her shabby treatment of the Chappell piano, Carlene Mair's booklet discusses the origins of the publishing business in sufficient detail, and informs us that around the year 1812, a certain Samuel Chappell entered into a business partnership with Francis Latour and John Cramer, the latter two being 'professors of music'. Piano manufacture appeared to be far from the minds of the three new partners at this early date; but the firm soon became involved in piano dealing, as Chappell's printed advertisement of 1812 announced:

'- - - - -*they have just opened a ware-room, for showing a number of instruments, consisting of grand, upright grand, square, cabinet and unique pianofortes etc. by the first makers.*' [2]

In 1819, Cramer withdrew from the partnership (he eventually founded his own publishing firm, J. B. Cramer and Company, in 1824); and in 1826, Latour also resigned his interest. By that date, Samuel Chappell the senior partner had moved the publishing house into premises at 50, New Bond Street. The firm was to remain at this address for the next one hundred and seventy years. Samuel died an early death in the year 1834. The business then passed into the hands of his widow, Emily, and her three young sons William, Thomas Patey, and Arthur. It was in fact Mrs Emily Chappell, reputedly quite a formidable lady, who took the bold step of instigating piano manufacture within the company. This happened at some point during the early 1840s, and the way it happened is quite interesting to observe.

Phoenix Street
The Chappell partners were too tied up with their demanding routine chores of publishing to consider becoming involved in the intricacies of piano construction, with all its technical headaches; but they did appear to have considerable capital to invest; and so Mrs Chappell arranged for the construction of a little piano factory in Phoenix Street, a short thoroughfare off the Charing Cross Road. The factory, of brick construction, was only forty-four feet long by thirty-five feet wide, but it had four floors, which was just about sufficient space to encompass a small workforce and also provide warehouse storage.[3] As the partners of the Chappell company knew nothing about piano making, they had to search for a master piano builder who would have all the skills necessary to be able to design and construct new instruments, who could hire the workforce, purchase all the required raw materials, and then take on the responsibility for the day-to-day running of the factory.

Luckily, they seem to have found these qualities in a certain Mr Smith, and ensconced him in Phoenix Street. All the instruments constructed under Smith's supervision in the little factory were made exclusively for Chappell, and 'as fast as he could finish the instruments they were taken by Messrs Chappell and Co. and were sold to the public by that firm.'[4] For the first fifteen years of production, the factory settled into a steady output of around five pianos per week.[5] The business arrangement worked in the following way: Chappell owned the factory building; Smith sold the completed instruments exclusively to Chappell, no doubt at a heavily-discounted 'trade' price, in view of the fact that he appears to have been provided with free manufacturing facilities; then the music publishers would profitably sell-on Smith's instruments at 50, New Bond Street, so recovering their investment in the factory building.

It is likely that piano making in Phoenix Street would have been carried out in the following way, which was something of a 'standard' arrangement for multi-storeyed piano-making workshops: soundboards and wooden braced backs were probably assembled on the top floor, and upon completion they would have been lowered (through a trapdoor) to the floor below. Here, the backs would have been strung up, and the veneered casework parts attached. Almost certainly, many of the casework components (such as carved legs or columns) would have been 'bought in' from local specialist sub-contractors. Lowered down to the floor below through another trapdoor, the pianos would have had their casework polished, and their actions and keyboards installed. The ground floor would have been a warehouse, where the completed instruments would have been checked over, tuned, and stored prior to their final despatch to New Bond Street. We can imagine Mr Smith's office being a grubby little cubbyhole, laden with paperwork, in this part of the building. He must have exhausted himself with the multitude of chores necessary to keep up with Chappell's constant demand.

A great tragedy befell the Phoenix Street workshops during the early hours of Sunday the 4th November 1860: the premises were burnt down in a terrible fire, caused by the over-heating of boiler pipes. The disaster, which killed one of the bystanders and injured a number of them, was reported in great detail in the pages of the *Morning Chronicle* of the following Tuesday. The following extract from the Chronicle's report gives some of the details:

'- - - -*Being something like 35 or 40 feet from the burning property, everyone naturally supposed that even if the walls should topple over they would be out of the way of danger. But judge of the consternation of the occupants of the Court* [Lloyd's Court, running along the back of the factory] *when all of a sudden, whilst eight or nine engines were at full play, and the men who were hired to work the engines were singing some lively airs, such as 'Up she rises early in the morning' and cries reverberating from the labourers of 'Beer, ho; beer, ho;' which nearly drowned the voices of the officers of the brigade, an explosion of terrible character took place - - - -*'

'- - - -*a piece of the steam piping, weighing about 56 pounds, was projected horizontally from the factory; the ponderous piece of machinery, after knocking away a portion of the arch of the side window, broke off and dropped about 2ft. 8in. of the iron work below into the court, whilst the remainder entered the window* [of a house in Lloyd's Court], *tore away a portion of the ceiling, perforated the partition and fell upon a bed in which a man was asleep, and actually setting on fire the sheets of the bed. The heated piping was pulled off the man, and he was rescued, much injured, but not fatally. - - - -*

- - - -The other portion of the iron piping, as before stated, fell into the court amongst several scores of persons. The first person it struck was a woman named Pitt, whose husband worked in an adjoining shop, and, hearing of the fire had hastened to see whether their own work was endangered, but finding such was not the case, they remained watching the spread of the flames. With such force was she struck that she was prostrated, and, upon being picked up by her husband, was found, in his opinion, to be mortally injured. He got her through the crowd the best way he could and had her placed in a conveyance, but while he was accompanying her to the hospital his worst fears were verified, and she died in his presence, before reaching the institution.' [6]

As a result of the conflagration, Mr Pitt was left in grief with six motherless children; Mr Smith lost around one hundred instruments in the course of construction; Chappell & Company lost their factory; piano production stopped abruptly; and Smith's skilled piano makers had to search for work elsewhere. We do not know how a supply of new instruments was maintained during the months following the fire. There must have been some source or other, because, according to the firm's serial numbers,[7] there was no decline in the numbers of Chappell pianos sold during the early 1860s. All that we do know is that Mr Smith's name disappears from involvement with piano production (we do not even know his first name) and that within a few years, Chappell had not only found new premises, but they had also entered into a manufacturing agreement with a new piano-making partnership. Perhaps the loss of the Phoenix Street factory did in fact mark the sad end of Smith's involvement in manufacture.

Belmont Street, Chalk Farm
Chappell's new factory was erected in Belmont Street, Chalk Farm Road, Camden Town, in what was then the outer suburbs of London, sometime around the years 1865-66. The factory still stands. By comparison with the Phoenix Street premises, the five-storey building is enormous, and dominates a considerable portion of the south side of the Street. There is also a huge yard to the rear of the premises, designed for use in the seasoning of tall stacks of timber. Chappell was to remain here for just over one hundred years, the factory premises being extended at various dates during this period. Around the year 1874, for example, a new three-storey block was constructed on the south end of the timber yard, facing towards Ferdinand Street. This new building, incorporating an arched entrance way for vehicles, eventually

The Chappell piano factory, main block, Belmont Street, Chalk Farm. Erected c.1865-66.
[Photo: David Thomas]

became the main access into the factory. The whole of the industrial complex became a famous local landmark, always known as Chappell's Piano Factory, although its occupier for its first thirty years was to be the manufacturing partnership of *Mugridge & Ulph*.

The founders of this partnership, a certain Thomas Shepheard Mugridge and a certain William Ulph, were very fortunate in achieving the tie-up with Chappell. (Whoever, for example, would wish to be the owner of a piano with the name *Mugridge & Ulph* proudly displayed on its nameboard?) The business agreement was formulated in much the same way as had been done earlier with Smith: Chappell & Company appear to have financed the construction of the factory, and the new partners occupied it in order to manufacture instruments exclusively for the music publishers to sell.

Thomas S. Mugridge (c1827-1895) was a native of Ashburton in Devonshire. By training he was a cabinet maker, not a piano constructor. He and his wife Elizabeth had arrived in London as a young married couple by the early 1850s. William Ulph (c1826-1902) came from the town of Aylsham in Norfolk, where his parents kept the *Red Lion* inn. William served an apprenticeship as a wheelwright, but like Mugridge, came up to London as a young man. Both of the new partners were essentially woodworkers, therefore, and appear to have had no practical knowledge of the important musical side of piano construction. Nevertheless, they must have had enough ambition and capital (particularly the latter) to have inspired the trust of Chappell & Co, who handed over the newly constructed premises for their use. The two partners are shown to be living in two managers' houses 'on site' in Belmont Street, according to the Census Return of 1871. In 1881 they were employing 109 men and 20 apprentices.[8] In the same year, output of Chappell pianos had increased to around twelve instruments per week, rising still further to around eighteen per week by the year 1890.

Work in progress at Chappell's factory, 1870. The tuner at the front right is 'chipping up' the strings of an upright piano. His colleague on the left appears to be polishing the outer casework of an upright.

[Heritage Image Partnership Ltd]

Thomas Mugridge saw to it that his two sons were fully trained in important aspects of piano manufacture. His eldest son, Thomas (c.1857-1906), was a piano stringer, tuner and voicer, and his younger son, William (born c.1860), became a piano action finisher and regulator. As children, the brothers would have played in and around the Chappell factory. Later on, as they became skilled in the most important aspects of piano construction, their knowledge would have complemented the woodworking abilities of their father and those of Ulph. We can be certain that Thomas Mugridge senior was hoping that his two sons would continue to run the business, and this must have been in his mind when he retired to Bishopsteignton in his native county of Devon, sometime between 1891 and 1893. He was to die there on the 3rd December 1895. In spite of all his industrious business activity over the previous thirty years, Mugridge was worth only some £300 on the day of his death.[9] This suggests that his enterprise with Ulph had not been an entirely successful one, from a financial point of view. (William Ulph, however, was worth £1,800 at the time of his death in March 1902.)

The unfolding events at Belmont Street during the 1890s may be best summarised by the following list:

1. Sometime between 1891 and summer 1893, Thomas Mugridge retired to Devon, and died there in 1895.

2. June 1893: Reinhold Friedrich Glandt moved into a house in Belmont Street, as the newly appointed factory manager. Mugridge & Ulph's business association with Chappell appears to have been terminated.

3. 1894: William Boosey began to succeed the Chappell brothers in the day-by-day administration of the firm, and there appears to have been an important change in company policy: the publishing house would no longer have its pianos made by contracted outworkers like Mugridge & Ulph, but would henceforth have direct control over piano manufacture in all its aspects.

4. 1895-96: piano output was drastically reduced to about half of what it had been in previous years. The cause of this serious disruption in production is presently unknown. There might have been a period of a few months when the factory actually lay unoccupied and dormant.

5. 1896: A Limited Liability company, covering both music publishing and piano making, was set up in December.

6. 1897: the second generation Mugridges, Thomas and William, still making pianos, but now trading from 15, Little Camden Street, Camden Town, became insolvent, and a receiving order was made against them on June 3rd. The loss of the regular Chappell business appears to have been a great blow to them.

7. 1897-1900: Output of pianos at Belmont Street regained its earlier 1891 level and then rapidly increased to over thirty per week during the year 1900. R.F. Glandt, continuing as factory manager, was appointed to the board of Chappell and became a director. From around this date, the piano manufacturing side of Chappell publishing began to exist as a separate business, known as *The Chappell Piano Company Ltd*.

R.F. Glandt

We must now turn to examine the highly important role that Glandt played in the evolution of the Chappell grand. The new models he designed and introduced at Belmont Street soon established the reputation of Chappell as makers of the finest concert instruments obtainable in this country. During the 1910 Promenade Season, for example, Chappell concert grands were used by eleven out of the twenty-one pianists appearing. Louis Bamberger, reminiscing around the year 1930, stated that Glandt was:

> - - - -*one of the greatest pianoforte makers ever connected with the British trade. He had the science as well as the practice of pianoforte construction. I believe he came from Poland and had learned his business in the Steinway factories. He was a very genial individual. After a time he told me he had been elected to the directorate of the Chappell Company. Unfortunately, both for the firm and himself, he was taken ill with an incurable disease. I remember visiting him in St Thomas's Hospital which he left shortly afterwards, but his ailment was incurable, and his passing away was a loss to the British pianoforte trade.*[10]

There is little doubt that R. F. Glandt was something of a genius. He was born at Kalisz, in Poland, on the 29th October 1840, and died in London on the 10th July 1902. The city of Kalisz was in fact the centre of Polish piano making. By trade, Glandt was originally a grand piano action finisher and regulator, but he gradually extended his knowledge and skill to become a piano scale designer and a maker of wooden foundry patterns. His ability to organise a piano factory must have been recognised by Chappell

Reinhold Friedrich Glandt (1840-1902).
[Photo: David Pescod family archive]

when they appointed him manager at the time of his removal into Belmont Street in the summer of 1893. He was certainly living and working in London by 1881, when the Census Return of that year shows him to be staying in a lodging house at 15, Duke Street, Marylebone.[11] He had married a German woman, Kathinka Bette, in 1877, and the couple produced three children: girls Elsa, Ida and Lilly.[12]

When Glandt applied for British citizenship in March 1900, his application documentation stated: 'Applicant has resided in England during the past 27 years'.[13] If this statement is indeed correct, it would mean that he had settled in London around the year 1873. Two of his daughters Elsa and Lilly, were born in London. This evidence begins to cast doubt on the statement that Glandt had 'learned his business in the Steinway factories', particularly as the Hamburg branch factory of that New York firm was not opened up until the year 1885, long after Glandt had settled in London. Nevertheless, it is quite possible that he might have spent a period of months working in the Steinway factory, offering his skills as a grand finisher and regulator.

The Chappell Piano Company commissioned Glandt to design four sizes of grand piano, and this time-consuming undertaking must have kept him very busy from the mid-1890s. The resulting models were known as the *Bijou* (exactly five feet long), the *Mignon* (exactly six feet long), the *Boudoir* (exactly seven feet) and the *Concert Grand* (eight foot nine inches long). All four models are distinguished by their decorative cast-iron frames, featuring attractive and intricate floral trellis work in the 'windows' found on the bentsides of each casting. (This is very much a German feature, found in the grands of Ibach of Barmen, for example.) It is presumed that Glandt, who was a proficient woodcarver as well as a skilled grand action mechanic, will have made the necessary wooden foundry patterns for these grand models himself.

The Norwich-based piano restorer, Ferguson Hoey, has worked on a number of Chappell concert grands from the Glandt period, and offers the following comments:

What has always struck me is the visual elegance of these instruments, the casework [rim] *beyond the keybed being extremely shallow* [in depth]. *The 'Art Nouveau' style windows in the domed casting* [iron frame] *are particularly pleasing. Alongside the Steinway 'D', the extreme treble tone might have seemed uncharacteristically weak. Most of the smaller Chappells seem to have plenty of 'zing' in the* [treble] *tonal make up, but I suspect that the concert models were a little thin* here. *Many pianists have remarked on the wonderful bass resonance of the Chappell: perfectly focused without 'sizzle', it seems to grow in depth and authority as one descends through the compass. The maple bass bridges are lightened, being relieved with large ovals, each with a saw cut from the bottom edge of the hole down onto the soundboard. This would afford a marked degree of flexibility along the bridge length - - - - a very clever bridge design. These were indeed noble instruments.*[14]

The 'weakness' in the high treble tone of the concert model was a flaw which Chappell acknowledged. For power and radiance of tone, their instruments simply could not compete with the equivalent Steinway in this region of the keyboard compass. (On the other hand, the Chappell concert model's top treble is no better or worse than any Bechstein concert grand of the same vintage.) Over thirty years after Glandt's introduction of the model, an attempt was made to improve the Chappell concert grand's top octave by a very curious method: instead of having the customary *three* strings per note here, the concert grand was given *four* strings for each individual note. This remodelling, done at some point during the 1930s, was carried out to the design of the factory manager, Ernest Gowland, whom we shall meet later on in this chapter. Apparently, the 'quadraphonic' stringing was not particularly successful in remedying the model's chronic top treble failings. The designs and patterns for Gowland's 'mark II' were destroyed by bombing during World War II, and so the Chappell company was obliged to revert to Glandt's original model, the wherewithal to manufacture this having survived the Blitz.

The Great War

The outbreak of the First World War had seen many of the Chappell workforce volunteer for trench warfare with Germany. According to a list of names printed in the October 1914 edition of *The Pianomaker* magazine, some sixty-one employees, perhaps almost one half of the workforce, had signed up for military service, either in Lord Kitchener's Army, or in the Territorials. Of these, thirty-eight sadly did not survive the War. Following the end of hostilities in 1918, an enamelled memorial plaque was raised up (applied to one of the outside walls of the factory within the factory yard) on which was inscribed the names of those employees killed on active service. Their names are shown in the list which appears in appendix 1.

The decimation of the Chappell workforce as a result of the First War must have been a terrible blow to the firm's morale. It was perhaps a response to this which prompted the Chappell directors to plan a move calculated to inspire confidence within the firm: they decided on an ambitious extension to the factory premises. This comprised a long, two-storey building, running down the side of the factory yard, which provided a link between the earliest five-storey premises in Belmont Street itself, and the later three-storey block facing Ferdinand Street. The extension, a quite ugly construction of steel girders and concrete (because of an acute shortage of bricks at the time) was opened on the 1st December 1920. The Opening Ceremony was performed by the famous concert pianist William Murdoch (1888-1942). All the Chappell employees attended. The edition of *The Pianomaker* magazine of the 15th December that year commented on the Ceremony as follows:

> *The gilded key and the silken cloth revealed a true sense of the importance of the development. Hundreds of workers assembled at the main entrance to greet the guests of the firm and closely followed each incident with a pleasurable interest that must be very gratifying to the directors and management of the Chappell Piano Co. Leading the way, Mr Murdoch, with Mr William Boosey, [the chairman of the company] entered the building, where a full-sized Concert Grand delighted the eyes and also later the musical senses of a highly-critical audience. Mr William Murdoch is, of course, the famous Australian pianist, who, together with artists like Lamond, Giloti and Moiselwitsch, have, as Mr Boosey said, 'sworn allegiance to the Chappell.' The liquid and full tone of the treble and tenor and the thunder of the bass of this Concert Grand was shown to the best advantage by Mr Murdoch in his two solos, which were rapturously applauded. Thereafter an extended tour was made of the factory buildings and proved, at any rate with regard to this firm, that a huge effort is being made to increase the quality and also the production in sufficient quantities of the British piano.*[15]

We are uncertain as to the exact purpose of Chappell's new extension, apart from its obvious function as an efficient and rain-proof link between the two older buildings. All we know is that the first floor of the new building actually has a sloping floor (sloping gradually downwards towards Ferdinand Street) which, it was claimed, helped the movement of pianos through the building during the stages of their construction. This idea, if a novel one, seems to us rather absurd! Was piano output accelerated as instruments were rapidly trundled down the slope? Were brakes necessary on the piano trolleys? The extension was certainly intended for a planned increase in piano output; but in actual fact, Chappell's production declined from 1920. Up to that year, a typical weekly output would have been around thirty instruments. Throughout the 1920s, Chappell's average weekly output never appeared to be more than twenty, declining still further in the early 1930s to no more than sixteen.[16] In the long run, it would appear that the extension proved to be quite unnecessary.

Reginald Neale

There was a young man, now sadly long-forgotten, 'working in the wings' at the Belmont Street factory, who made notable improvements to the tonal qualities of Chappell uprights during the early 1920s. He was Reginald George Neale (1901-1926). At the age of fourteen, in 1915, Neale was apprenticed to the firm of Allison, where he was given the opportunity to experiment with the 'scaling' (the design of string length, thickness and tension) of instruments then in production. The result of his work was a decided improvement to the sound of the Allison piano. During his apprenticeship, Neale had the benefit of studying the complexities of piano design under Sydney Hurren at the Trades School within the Northern Polytechnic.

In 1921, at the age of only twenty, he was taken on by the Chappell Piano Company and given the important role of designing new upright models from the drawing board. Whilst employed at Chappell, Neale was awarded a *Federation Travelling Scholarship* which enabled him to study piano design and construction in piano factories in France, Belgium and Germany. Sadly, 'Reg' Neale became seriously ill, and died as a result of tuberculosis and meningitis on the 9th November 1926, aged only twenty-five. His death was regarded as a terrible loss to the London piano industry.[17] We are not exactly certain which new Chappell models emerged as a result of his time spent at Belmont Street. One of them might have been the well-known *Elysian* upright, the frame and scale of which later became the basis of the Chappell 'school' model; but the overall improvements to the tonal qualities of the Chappell upright instruments from the early 1920s, as a result of Neale's endeavours, were certainly long-remembered within the Trade.[18]

Ernest Gowland

In February 1926, the Chappell Piano Company appointed a new factory manager and technical director, Ernest Gowland (c.1879-1950). This individual came from a line of distinguished piano makers particularly associated with the Hopkinson company.[19] His grandfather, Edward 'Big' Gowland (so named to distinguish him from his son, also named Edward, who must have been of smaller stature!) was for many years foreman of Hopkinson's London factory. Edward 'the Big' is credited with the invention of the 'pressure bar' in the upright piano in the year 1872. Ernest Gowland, Edward's grandson, joined the famous firm of George Rogers & Sons in 1915, and had become Rogers' factory manager by July 1920. During the early 1920s, he was involved in the scale design of a number of successful new Rogers upright instruments, together with one baby grand. There is an important curiosity we must remember about all these new models: Gowland, always known to be an astute businessman, and a crafty one perhaps, retained a personal ownership to all his designs: they never appear to have belonged to the Rogers company.

In December 1925, he resigned from his post at Rogers, to be replaced as technical director there by John Challen, who had recently been manager of the ailing Charles Challen & Son.[20] Two months later, Gowland entered the Chappell factory, bringing his piano designs with him. He soon withdrew from production most of the existing Chappell upright models, and replaced them with those recently made to his own designs at Rogers. In October 1926, for example, the *Diamond* upright was introduced, followed by the *Emerald* upright (May 1927) and then by the *Pearl* baby grand (July 1927).[21] All these models had recently been made as Rogers pianos! And so we can suggest that many of the Chappell uprights made from 1926, and the one baby grand, were identically sounding instruments to the Rogers models of a slightly earlier date. It is likely that Gowland will have continued to receive some kind of royalty payment for the continued use of his own designs at Chappell.

Ernest Gowland (c.1879-1950).
[Photo: Michael Vivien family archive]

Once he had established himself at Belmont Street, Gowland achieved a reputation as a money lender to the workforce: those individuals who ran out of cash before the weekly pay packet arrived, would approach Gowland for a short-term loan, which he would willingly provide; but when any indebted worker was paid his wage, Gowland would charge an exorbitant amount of interest! Although his obvious technical skills were greatly admired throughout the industry, he nevertheless must have been intensely disliked by some of the Chappell factory staff.

An event of major importance to Chappell occurred in June 1929: the old-established company changed ownership, and was taken over by an American music-publishing consortium headed by Louis Dreyfus and his brother Max. As a result of the takeover, Chappells became agents for a wide range of highly popular music publications emanating from America, such as the material of Rodgers and Hammerstein, Rodgers and Hart, or Lerner and Lowe. And also as a result of the take-over, fresh capital was introduced into the firm, which certainly was of benefit to the piano manufacturing side of the London business. Not only did the fresh capital help Chappell's piano making survive the very difficult years for the Trade during the late 1920s and early 1930s: it also enabled Chappell to purchase the goodwill of two other London manufacturers: Allison, and Collard & Collard (both acquired in 1929).[22]

A perusal through a Chappell piano sales brochure and price list surviving from October 1929 will give a very good indication of the product line offered at that date.[23] The three largest grands available (*concert, 7' boudoir* and *6' mignon*) were the original Glandt models dating from the late 1890s; but Glandt's 5' baby grand (the *Bijou*) had been withdrawn, and was replaced by another grand, the '5' 3''', a completely-new Gowland design. To these four was added the *Pearl* baby grand (4' 6" long), the design for which Gowland had materialised from Rogers. New Gowland-designed upright models were introduced as the 1930s progressed, whilst the quantity of the larger grands made appears to have shrunk (the 7' model was eventually discontinued, for example). The uprights became shorter and shorter – as it became seemingly essential for the industry's survival to meet the public's demand for more compact models for the home. By the late 1930s, the tallest and most expensive Chappell upright, the model 'C', was only 3' 11" in height (119cm). Two even smaller grands were launched in 1937: a baby of only 4' 4" length (132cm), and an even smaller baby of an almost ridiculous 4' length (122cm). (For Chappell prices, October 1929, see appendix 2.)

A piano technician, the late Percy Cossins, who had worked at the Chappell factory during the 1930s, wrote to the author in May 1987 with the following interesting story about one particular 5' 3" model:

> Our 5' 3" Bijou was quite nice. I had one especially prepared for my own use. In its time it was used for concerts and festivals [at Scunthorpe] – and even came to the rescue for a special two-piano concert with Rawicz and Landauer: we were promised two Steinway concert grands but only one turned up; we balanced up the Chappell to the Steinway with mikes, and believe it or not, giving good reception throughout the Theatre – and best of all the pianists were quite happy![24]

The Chappell 'Blüthner'
There was a curious incident involving the Chappell factory in early 1935, which certainly needs to be recorded as part of north London's 'folk history' of piano making:

In the early 1930s, the German Blüthner company of Leipzig had introduced a baby grand, the model '4', of length 4' 11" (150cm). This newly-designed instrument was selling very well in piano shops, particularly in Blüthner's own showrooms in Wigmore Street, London. The highly successful sales of this particular model had become very much the envy of other quality manufacturers, such as Chappell. Successful sales were due in part to the 'lustre' of the Blüthner name. The piano was also very well designed, with a light and responsive action, and clear sounding and sonorous middle and treble registers. Only the bass section is 'lacking', the result of too short string lengths and a bass bridge which is too close to the edge of the soundboard. The Chappell factory was ordered to make a perfect carbon copy of this instrument.

The piano makers of Belmont Street must have shaken their heads in disbelief when given these instructions. They knew quite well that the firm's own 5' 3" Bijou model was just as good as any model 4 Blüthner. Nevertheless, instructions had to be obeyed, and so an example of the little Blüthner grand was smuggled into the factory, where it was dutifully

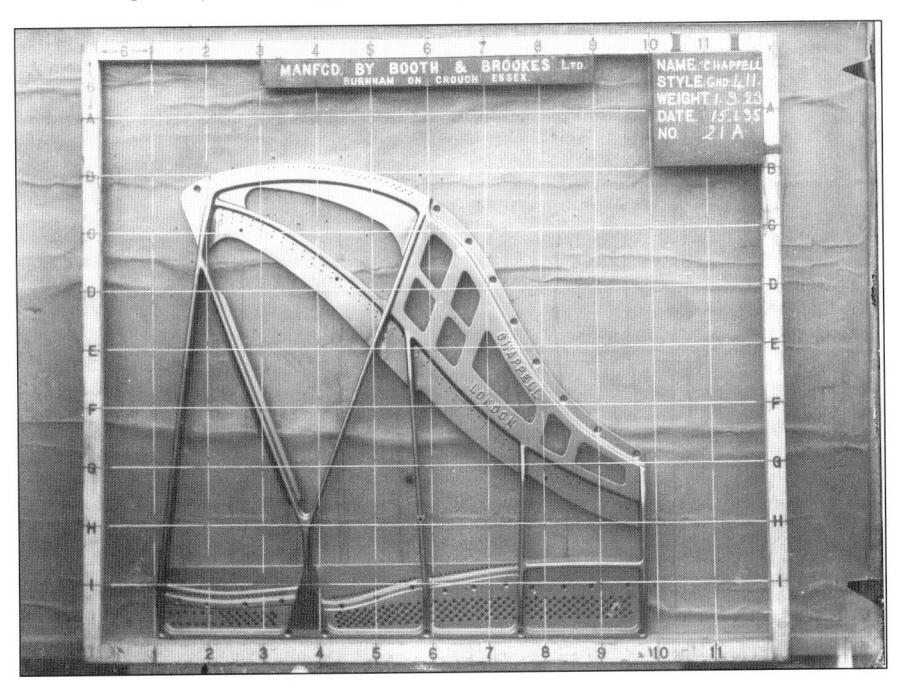

The cast-iron frame for the Chappell 'Blüthner' grand.
[Booth & Brookes ironfoundry archives, Essex County Record Office, Chelmsford]

measured up and ultimately dismantled. Every small part of the instrument was painstakingly copied, including the distinctive Blüthner style of the cast-iron frame. Then a prototype 'clone' was constructed, and the directors arrived for their eagerly-awaited inspection. The new piano sounded nothing like a Blüthner! Nevertheless, the model went into regular production, and was offered to the public along with other similar-sized Chappell grands.[25]

The Closing Years
The wartime bombing and destruction of the Chappell-owned Queen's Hall, during one night of the Blitz in June 1941, seems to have marked the end of Chappell's regular involvement in the supply of concert grands for leading London halls; and the War itself almost completely stopped the manufacture of instruments from Belmont Street: output was reduced to a trickle, or not at all. Between 1942 and 1947, for example, an average of no more than two instruments per week left the premises. Production picked up in 1948, when about eight instruments were dispatched on a weekly basis; but then throughout the 1950s, output averaged out at around six each week, or one piano for each working day, a significant decline when compared with the 1930s level of production.[26] The workforce was decreasing in numbers, but increasing in age.

When the author of this book visited the factory as a young man on a hot summer's day in 1963, he noted that the average age of the Chappell craftsman was sixty years or over. The three-storey Ferdinand Street building was unused, apart from the manager's office; and the five-storey building in Belmont Street was manned by no more than about ten individuals. This meant that huge areas of floor space were empty and unoccupied, with just an occasional worker active in one odd corner or another. Two charming, elderly grey-haired gentlemen were responsible for 'bellying' (soundboard making) on the ground floor; there was but one tuner on the premises, and only one upright action finisher to be seen. The very elderly and semi-retired grand finisher, Ralph Ralphs,

Ralph Ralphs (c.1881-1975).
[Photo: Mary and James MacLauchlan family archive]

came in a couple of days each week, just to keep grand production ticking over.[27] It was almost a 'token' workforce. Clearly, the piano-manufacturing side of Chappell had suffered from a great deal of neglect and disinterest from the management in New Bond Street. The factory seemed to the author almost like a 'forgotten', fossilised phenomenon, locked in a time warp. He felt almost privileged to have witnessed for a short time the slow twilight of this once-great manufacturing enterprise.

During his visit, the author was taken into the single-storeyed grand rim bending shop, situated in the outside yard. There, he saw an impressive but sad sight: row upon row of grand presses – perhaps a dozen of them in a row – the majority of them overwhelmed and choked with cobwebs. Only one solitary press, to make the rim of one of the smallest of the grands, appeared to be in regular use. Chappell had clearly long given-up the manufacture of larger grands for professional concert use.

The music publishing and piano making firm of Chappell was taken over by the Dutch enterprise, Phillips Electrical, in 1970. The Phillips directors must have been quite amazed when they inspected their antique piano factory shortly after their purchase. They ordered its immediate closure. The few surviving craftsmen in the factory were then determined not to let anything survive which might be of use to any other piano manufacturer: they wilfully broke up the dozens of jigs and templates and, along with all the scale drawings and various foundry patterns, burnt them on the factory boiler. When other piano manufacturers (Alfred Knight, for example) descended, vulture like, to attend the closing auction at the factory, they were disappointed to discover that all that appeared to be left was a small stock of seasoning timber and some woodworking machinery.

The impressive Chappell factory survives to this day, a landmark in the Camden Town district. It has been threatened with demolition, but a local public enquiry held in early 2011, following a campaign by local councillors and a petition signed by many local residents, saved the building.[28] The latest plans are to remodel the premises and turn them into offices or dwelling flats. Let us hope that future occupiers of the buildings will remember that this former factory once turned out the finest concert grands ever made in this country, and as such, made a significant and worthy contribution to the musical culture of the nation.

2
EAVESTAFF, BRASTED BROTHERS AND THE *MINIPIANO*

THIS chapter deals with a period of piano making in London involving the Eavestaff and Brasted companies, and with the origin and evolution of a little keyboard novelty which at the time was thought to have 'saved' the British piano industry from almost total collapse during the 1930s: the 'minipiano'. We are looking at three distinct phases of history: first, that of the original Eavestaff company, founded in London in the year 1823 by William Eavestaff; secondly, the takeover of the same company almost one hundred years later, in October 1920, by the Brasted brothers; and thirdly, the manufacture by Brasteds, from 1934, of newly designed minipianos, the vast majority of them bearing the time-honoured Eavestaff name.

Eavestaff origins

The founder of the Eavestaff concern, a certain William Eavestaff (born circa 1791) had married eighteen-year-old Hannah Pontifex in 1815. Three years later, their child William Glen was born. (The unusual middle name 'Glen' came from William Glen's grandfather, Glen Eavestaff. We wonder if there was in fact a possible family connection with the certain Mr Glen, who was Broadwood's chief outdoor piano tuner around the year 1800.) In the course of time, William Glen Eavestaff succeeded to his father's business and took two of his sons into partnership, so that the firm became styled *W. G. Eavestaff & Sons*. William Glen was always known as 'young Eavestaff' to distinguish him from his father, a title which stuck with him even when he became elderly, but still active in the business.

The Eavestaff factory was originally in Euston Road. By the end of the nineteenth century, the company had opened prestigious showrooms and offices in Berners Street, just to the north of Oxford Street. By the year 1911, the firm had moved showrooms to 38, Baker Street, and the factory was relocated in Salusbury Road, Kilburn, north-west London. Our knowledge of the company's activities during the nineteenth century is unfortunately very limited: Victorian pianos bearing the name 'Eavestaff' never seem to materialise in the sale rooms, and piano tuners do not appear to come across them on their rounds. This leads us to speculate that the company might have been, like many other piano makers in London at the time, primarily a 'trade' manufacturer, whose pianos would bear the names of regional piano shops, or even carry bogus German names. One such firm, for example, Godfrey & Company, chose to make pianos with the fictitious German name *Waldstein* attached. Whatever the label appearing on any Eavestaff product, the makers had a reputation for manufacturing a highly-dependable musical instrument at an affordable price. As far as we are aware, the original company never made grands, but only concentrated on uprights.

William G. Eavestaff was frequently visited at his Berners Street premises by Louis Bamberger, a dealer in soundboard wood who was looking for business. Bamberger, writing many years later, had this to say about him:

I have vivid recollections of W. G. Eavestaff of Berners Street. His factory was in the Euston Road. He had a fine old class of business and he did know how to make a piano. It was his custom to spend an hour or two over lunch each day in his room over his shop in Berners Street. One knew exactly the time to catch him. I remember how he used to come down those stairs. He extended to you a most gracious welcome, and always asked, 'Do I owe you any money? If I do, I will now discharge your debt'. He was most punctual. Afterwards he would talk and as he was most punctilious in the final looking over of each pianoforte before it left the factory, he would remark: 'My people at the factory think that I am a damn old fool, but I know my work, and I won't allow anything to go out which is not up to my standard.'[1]

What Louis Bamberger may not have realised is that old William was probably approaching his ninetieth year when he met him. This would be the simple explanation for the maker's need for an hour or two's rest (and probably a snooze!) each lunch time. William Glen Eavestaff died on the 10th February 1912, aged ninety-four. He was worth some £6,000 at the time of his death, and so was quite comfortably 'well off' by the standards of the day.[2]

His successors were two of his sons, William junior and Frank Leonard Eavestaff, both of whom are likely to have been trained in their father's factory in order to gain practical knowledge of piano making. The elder of the two, William (c.1858-1917), lived in St John's Wood, married later in life, died aged fifty-nine, but had no children who might have continued the family business. His much younger brother Frank (c.1876-1957) had one child, a daughter. He appeared reluctant to remain in sole charge of the family firm. At the age of about forty-four, three years after his brother's death, Frank sold the Eavestaff concern to H.F. & R.A. Brasted (October 1920) and eventually retired to Hastings, Sussex, although there is evidence to show that he was still involved in manufacturing into the early 1920s, possibly as a consultant to help smooth over the continuity from Eavestaff to Brasted.[3] Certainly Eavestaff's own factory in Salusbury Road, Kilburn, was maintained for at least four years following the Brasted take over, and Frank may have continued to work there throughout this period.

Brasted of Hackney

The Brasted company had been founded by Henry George Brasted (1851-1908), a Londoner, in the year 1870. He was the first member of his family to be involved in the piano industry – his forebears had been haberdashers and mercers for a number of generations.[4] Henry was trained as a piano tuner, and immediately upon the completion of his apprenticeship, at the age of nineteen and full of ambition, he set up his own piano tuning business. He is described as a 'piano tuner' in the London Census Returns of 1881, by which date he was living at 76, Potterscroft Road, Hackney, and had recently married a Yorkshire woman, Julia Wright from Goole. The couple raised a family of four sons and two daughters. All four of the sons, and one of the daughters, were to follow in their father's footsteps in the piano industry. (For an outline tree of the Brasted family, see appendix 3.)

Like the third William Eavestaff, Henry Brasted was to die in his fifties, at the age of fifty-seven, in 1908. By this date, he had developed a small but successful piano-making concern at 38-40, Upper Clapton Road, Hackney, unashamedly manufacturing 'trade' instruments, on to which a variety of names could be affixed – either the names of the music shops from which any Brasted piano would ultimately be purchased, or names chosen from a medley of fanciful, evocative ones, suggestive of quality and culture. For example, the Brasted pianos which were supplied to the retailers Wigmore

RESPONSIBILITY

THE manufacturers of Brasted Pianos do not for a moment forget their responsibility as the makers of a piano which has maintained such a high standard for so long.

They jealously guard, not only their own reputation, but those of thousands of dealers who are identified with the name of Brasted.

That is why nothing but the finest materials, the most skilled labour are employed; and every piano which leaves the Brasted factories undergoes a series of vigorous tests.

Brasted Pianos build reputations—and maintain them. Your name on a Brasted Piano is a guarantee of rapidly increasing business.

BRASTED

H. F. & R. A. BRASTED

Piano Manufacturers

38-40 UPPER CLAPTON ROAD, LONDON, E.5.

Brasted Brothers' advertisement in **The Pianomaker** *magazine, March 1921.*
[Author's collection]

Hall Piano Galleries, west London, bore either the names *Wigmore* or *Welbeck* above their keyboards. Other brand names frequently used by Brasted include *Bannerman*, *Cumberland*, *Dorchester*, *Paul Gerard* and *Reger*. Instruments with the latter name attached were supplied exclusively to Harrods; and the proud owner of a new *Dorchester* model upright in his or her very modest living room might have felt secure in the knowledge that their new acquisition appeared to have some association or other with an exclusive London hotel. Brasted's advertisement in the Trade magazine, *The Pianomaker*, of March 1921, informed the retailers: 'Your name on a Brasted piano is a guarantee of rapidly increasing business'.

At the time of Henry Brasted's early death in 1908, his four sons, Henry Charles, Frederick Elliott, Robert Percy and Albert George, were all working in the family business. The brothers were in their twenties: Henry, the eldest (known as 'Harry'), was twenty-eight in 1908; the youngest, Albert (known as 'Bert'), was twenty-four. Each brother had a particular responsibility within the firm: Harry was in charge of production, and had a high level of manual skill; Robert (who was usually known in the Trade by his second name, Percy) had clerical skills and handled the commercial and financial side of the business. The youngest brother, Bert, was responsible for sales, and travelled the length and breadth of the country promoting the firm's products. Sadly, the third brother, Frederick, was killed during World War I as a result of an explosion.

The three surviving brothers made an excellent team, one brother's talents complementing another's. But we must not forget the role played by their sister Hilda Lenora, who became company secretary and who worked full-time in the office, helping to maintain an efficient administration in what was to become a rapidly growing concern. During the early 1920s, the firm was styled *H.F. & R.A. Brasted* (a rather confusing title, as it suggests that only two partners were involved, whereas each initial stood for one particular brother, in order of seniority). By the 1930s, the firm, now a registered limited company, had gained the less cumbersome title of *Brasted Brothers Ltd*.

Brasted acquires Eavestaff
As we have previously noted, it was in October 1920 that the Brasted brothers acquired the old-established firm of W.G. Eavestaff & Sons. The benefit to them was twofold: first of all, it enabled them to place the time-honoured name *Eavestaff* on to some of their products, so helping to gain sales and to help inspire confidence within the Trade, which would have been very familiar with the Eavestaff product; and secondly, the company is likely to

have acquired an input of valuable skill from Eavestaff craftsmen. The purchase was certainly a bold venture for the brothers, particularly in the year 1920 when the very high cost of post-War materials made pianos expensive and hard to sell. It was certainly a difficult time for the industry. A number of long-established and reputable manufacturers, whose pianos had become household names, were now struggling to survive. John Brinsmead & Sons, once a brilliantly successful enterprise, succumbed to the liquidator in the spring of 1921. The highly respected J. & J. Hopkinson collapsed in January 1924. In March 1926, the old-established but ailing Charles Challen & Son was offered for sale. If, like so many others in the industry at that date, the original Eavestaff firm was struggling to survive, then the Brasted brothers are likely to have picked up the business for a very reasonable price.

Whatever the cost of the purchase, and the risks involved, we do know that the brothers were soon ready to commit themselves to a huge expansion in output: in the spring of 1923, they vacated their old premises at Upper Clapton Road and moved to a 'greenfield' site in Hermitage Road, Harringay, north London, where a range of single-storey buildings was erected. It is likely that a proportion of the skilled Eavestaff staff from Kilburn joined them there. The new factory was considered to be the largest piano workshop in the country, and a promotional print which appeared in an advert of April 1924 certainly suggests this to have been the case,[5] although many of the buildings, being single storey sheds, give an overall impression of a shanty town, built hurriedly and at minimal cost. Nevertheless, the production facilities, now covering 27,000 square feet of ground-floor space, must have significantly increased manufacturing efficiency, and eased expansion of output. The firm of Brasted was to remain here for the next forty-seven years. Its long-held

The Brasted 'Dorchester' upright in a figured walnut case, c.1930.
[Author's collection]

claim that its factory was the largest of its kind in the country remained undisputed through to the mid-1960s. It was also once regarded as the largest of its kind in Europe.[6]

It is very hard to estimate the true level of output at Hermitage Road, as serial numbers found in pianos can be misleading, (and some manufacturers even went so far as to fictitiously 'make them up' to make it appear to the unsuspecting public that their output was much greater than it really was!) At the same time, new ranges of instruments by the same manufacturer (such as the minipianos) often have their own set of serial numbers, complicating the issue even further. But using the available serial numbers as a rough guide,[7] we can estimate that the Brasted workshops might have been turning out something like fifty new pianos per week by the late 1920s, with a rise in production level to perhaps something approaching one hundred per week by the early 1930s, rising still further to a staggering two hundred per week by the late 1930s, once minipiano production was in full swing.

The original minipiano of Erbe Maas

Having introduced the Eavestaff and Brasted firms, we can now turn our attention to the minipiano, and take a look at its origins. We know the name of the individual who is credited with the design of the *original* minipiano: he was in fact a Dutchman, a certain Ludwig Maas, who was working as factory manager for the German piano manufacturers, J. Erbe, of Eisenach. The earliest examples of the original minipiano were constructed in Erbe's Eisenach factory from around the year 1924. This original model has every feature found in the earliest minipianos made in London, as we shall discuss shortly.

Surprisingly, the original 'minipiano' was seen in London in May 1929: the design had been licensed by Erbe to Henry Hicks and Son, an old-established south London firm, for Hicks to copy and build. But for some reason, the product never 'caught on', and Hicks dropped the project shortly afterwards – perhaps because the manufacture of such a quirky item proved troublesome. In 1929, the cast-iron frames for the mini were being produced at Booth and Brookes' iron foundry, Burnham-on-Crouch, Essex.[8]

The original 'mini' (as we shall now call it) has a number of highly distinctive features, which deserve to be noted:

1. The instrument is extremely small in height: only 84cm (2 feet 9 inches), making it perhaps the most diminutive upright piano ever

seen. With its keyboard compass of only six octaves instead of the customary seven, it is a highly compact piece of furniture, and contrasts very much with the taller and bulkier uprights which were much more typical of the 1920s.
2. The stringing is a mixture of monocords (only one string per note) for the first thirty-five notes of the keyboard compass (low bass 'F' up to D♯ above middle C), then bicord (two strings per note) for the remaining thirty-eight notes, up to the high treble 'F'. This compares with the usual three strings for most notes (tricord) found in all other pianos of the period. The mini has the usual 'overstrung' scale, in which the wound bass strings cross diagonally in front of the remaining strings.
3. The foundation of the mini's structure is a light 'all over' cast-iron frame which dispenses with the need for any wooden back bracings, so simplifying construction and reducing manufacturing costs.
4. The most radical and unconventional feature of the design is the fact that the action is at the *rear* of the piano, *behind* the stringing and the soundboard. The hammers therefore strike the strings in the direction *towards* the player. The keyboard and key frame are balanced on the upper flanged edge of the iron frame, and connection to the action at the rear of the instrument is by means of slim linkage rods.
5. The soundboard faces into the room, at the front of the instrument, under the keyboard, and in the close vicinity of the player's knees. The forward surface of the board is veneered all over, to appear like the 'bottom door' of a conventional piano. Unusually, and as a space-saving device, the soundboard ribs and its two bridges are attached to the one (rear) side of the soundboard. These highly original features are better explained in the accompanying photographs.
6. The tuning pins, of unusually long length and specially manufactured, are located immediately *underneath* the keyboard, and pass right through the tuning plank to the other side of the piano, where they hold the strings up to tension.
7. The case design is very minimal and spartan, with absolutely no superficial decoration or ornamentation – no doubt in an attempt to keep manufacturing costs to a bare minimum. In order to help maintain its diminutive height, the piano is not provided with a set of castor wheels.

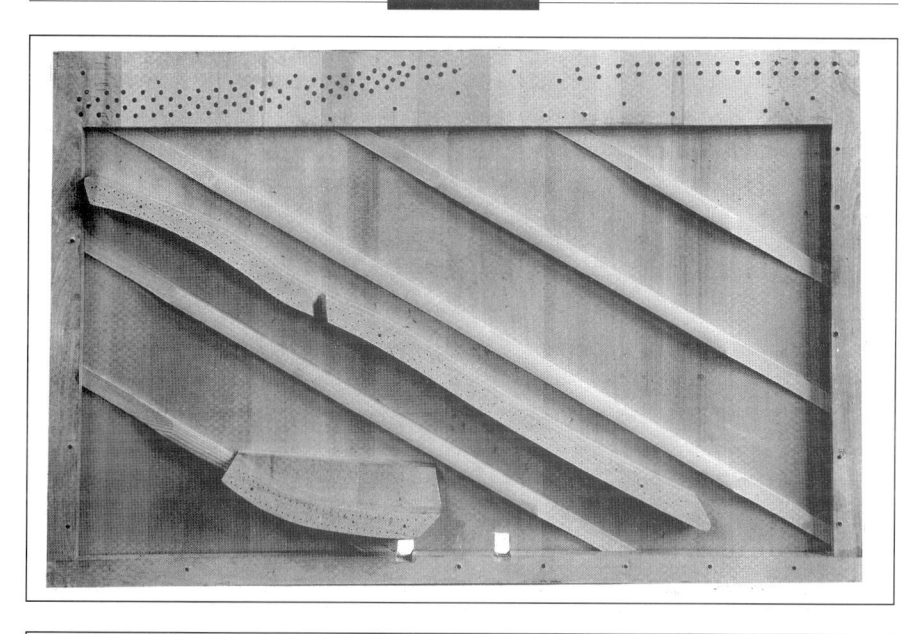

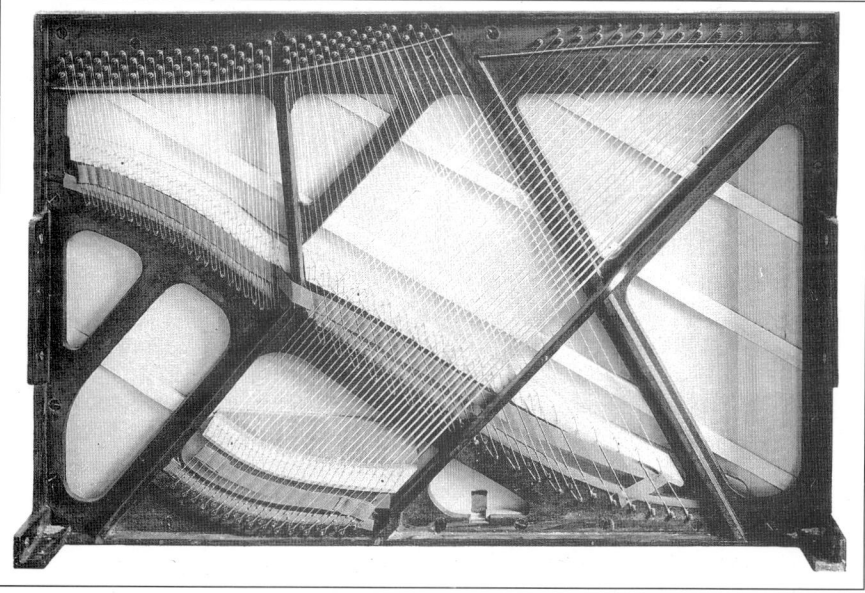

EAVESTAFF, BRASTED BROTHERS AND THE *MINIPIANO* 27

The back of the 'original' mini piano, as made by Erbe Maas of Eisenach, Germany. The upper photo shows the highly unusual feature of ribs and bridges placed together on the same side of the soundboard. The lower photo shows the cast-iron frame and stringing now attached.
[Author's collection]

The greatest attraction of such a piano is its extremely compact form, a very welcome feature for any purchaser occupying a smaller home, or even dwelling in a caravan. Its affordability was of course another, most attractive, feature: the mini as later made by Brasted Brothers Ltd would have sold in piano shops at about half the price of the large, conventional English uprights by Broadwood, Chappell, Marshall & Rose or Rogers. Tonally, the original mini has a degree of attractiveness as well: its sound is bright, clear, fresh, and surprisingly loud and sustained for such a compact design – mainly as a result of the location of the soundboard, which projects the piano's sound directly into the room, rather than towards the wall behind the instrument. Understandably, because of the use of monocord stringing, the original mini lacks any real strength or power in its bass and tenor registers.

The new design received a mixed reception from technicians in the piano industry. The instrument was highly irritating to tune, as the tuner had to kneel piously in front of the piano, on a cushion on the floor, in order to see the tuning pins inconveniently placed under the keyboard. This could be highly uncomfortable and embarrassing, especially for older and less agile members of the profession, or for blind tuners; and then at the same time he or she would have to stretch themselves forward, towards the out-of-sight rear of the piano, in a desperate struggle to try and gain access to the stringing, into which the tuning muting wedges would need to be placed. It was even suggested that the tuner ought to have been some kind of 'contortionist' in order to successfully carry out a tuning!

Nevertheless, the novel product was enthusiastically received by the music profession, but usually from musicians in the light music field, where a much smaller and less obtrusive upright, perhaps electrically amplified, was a welcome feature on a variety bandstand or in a pit orchestra. The following testimonials were received by Eavestaff/Brasted, shortly after they had introduced their own version of the mini:

Jack Hylton: *For an instrument of such small proportions, the tone and volume of the Minipiano is extraordinary.*

Jack Payne: *The Minipiano has amazing tone for so small an instrument.*

Ambrose: *The Minipiano appeals to me from every angle.*

Gracie Fields: *I suppose I am expected to pay tribute to the beautiful tone of the Minipiano, as indeed I do, but what strikes me most is the delightful design and artistic colours.*

Mantovani: *Every now and then I come across an instrument which fills me with a complete sense of satisfaction. I had that feeling when I first made the acquaintance of the Minipiano. It has a fascination all of its own, both in performance and appearance.*[9]

What is conspicuous by its absence, is a testimonial or recommendation from any leading concert pianist, whose opinion would have been highly respected. Either the 'serious' concert pianists of the day were never approached for an opinion, or perhaps with their eyes on the public concert hall, they simply could not appreciate the usefulness and attractiveness of the mini to an ordinary household.

Percy Brasted

The Brasted-owned Eavestaff company entered the minipiano field in early 1934. At this date, it was discovered that the original version of the model was now being made in Stockholm, Sweden, by the firm of C.A.V. Lundholm. It appeared that Lundholm had purchased the design from the first German manufacturer, Erbe. Percy Brasted, who was the one of the three brothers with a particular interest in developing the mini, perceived the huge potential commercial value of the design, and was keen to make it at Hermitage Road. In fact, it was Percy who coined the title 'minipiano', and went as far as to register it as a trademark. He negotiated with Lundholm to purchase, lock stock and barrel, all the manufacturing rights, designs, drawings, jigs and templates necessary to make the product in London; but it was agreed that a number of minis bearing the Lundholm name would continue to be made for export to the firm in Sweden.

Percy Brasted (1882-1954).
[Photo: Robert Brasted family archive]

During the first nine months of English production, some 1,500 new pianos, the vast majority of them minis bearing either the *Eavestaff* or *Lundholm* name, were turned out, indicating a production of approximately forty instruments per week. By February 1936, the total number of pianos produced at Hermitage Road had reached 6,386; by December 1937: 8,500; and by June 1938, the remarkable figure of 10,396.[10] On the 27th October 1935, Percy Brasted sailed from Southampton to New York, a trip partly for pleasure, but, ever ambitious, Percy was also engaged in negotiations with the New York firm of Hardman Peck to have even more minis made under licence in the USA. He returned to England from his trip in March the following year.

In spite of the obvious commercial success of the mini, the new and novel product had a number of recognised shortcomings: the difficulties of coping with the tuning caused considerable criticism; the tonal weakness of the monochord and bicord stringing was acknowledged; and the limitations of the narrow keyboard compass of only six octaves were recognised. These defects began to be eliminated from May 1936, when the first of a series of evolved minis was introduced. The 'mark II' was slightly taller than the original version, by some six inches (15cm). The action was moved from the back of the instrument to its conventional location at the front, and so tuning irritation was solved at a stroke. During the period 1938-40, further versions were introduced: the compass of the mini model was extended to the standard seven octaves, then to seven-and-one-quarter octaves, and tricord stringing replaced bicord. By the year 1940, the mini had a fuller and more rounded tone quality, and the enlarged keyboard compass enabled a much wider repertoire of music to be played upon it.

These various versions of the mini were served up in a wide variety of casework styles, offering an attractive choice to any customer tempted to consider a purchase. The basic template style is described in brochures as *The Modern* (see illustration), with a variant on this design having panelled ends, and called *The Period*. The *Hanover* model has curved cabriole legs attached in front; the *Tudor* features even more panelling, a token amount of wood carving, and is built in oak; and finally the casework of the most expensive *De Luxe* model boasts a glossy ebonised case, 'Art Deco' chrome strips, and novel electrical lights mounted on the top of each case end. Every mini was available in a bewildering range of veneers, colours or finishes: birch ply, mahogany, walnut, ebonised (black), or enamelled in white, cream, black or green. The finish could be 'satin', 'crackle', or a purchaser might choose to indulge in a mirror-like full gloss polish. At the same time as the evolved versions of the minipiano were introduced, Brasted brothers decided to continue with production of the original six-octave Erbe-Mass version, also available in a range of finishes, but somewhat illogically, called the *Eavestaff Ritz*.

Jack Davis

The individual who must have received enormous gratitude from the Brasted brothers for the internal technical improvements which created the later evolved minis, was a senior employee, John Thomas Davis (1899-1977), who

EAVESTAFF, BRASTED BROTHERS AND THE *MINIPIANO* 31

The upper photo shows an Eavestaff mini piano in a mahogany case with matching stool, c.1950. The lower photo shows the strung back for the same piano, in production from 1940 and designed by Jack Davis. The beginnings of 'extended overstringing' can be seen.
[Photos: Author's collection]

had worked in a technical capacity with the firm from 1924. Known in the Trade as 'Jack' Davis, he was a highly skilled piano scale designer, and very much a 'self-educated' man, with an extraordinary wide and deep knowledge of piano history, design and manufacture.[11] He was a founder member of the Institute of Musical Instrument Technology in 1938, and gave lectures to that Institute. He was still to be found at the Hermitage Road works over thirty-five years later, distinguished-looking, white-haired and dressed in immaculate white overalls, continuing to make modifications to the design of the models then in production, whilst at the same time working on the prototype of the *Minitronic* (see page 36).

It could be rightly claimed that Jack Davis was on something of a 'learning curve' when it came to his involvement in the evolution of the internal design of the Eavestaff mini. Each new design he introduced or adopted was usually an improvement, in some way or other, on an earlier version of the same. It is estimated that Davis must have been responsible for overseeing the introduction of about eleven new designs of piano (minis, conventional uprights, and grands) during his time with Brasted.

John 'Jack' Davis and his wife Lillian, c.1970.
[Photo: John A. Davis family archive]

Our most interesting discovery, after analysing and comparing each of the mini designs, is the way that the length of the bass strings in each model is gradually increased, so that in Davis's later designs, the overstringing extends diagonally from one extreme corner of the iron frame to the far opposite corner. It was claimed (and verified by measurement) that Davis's longest mini bass strings were equal in length to those found in a 5-foot grand. He also experimented with actions, and introduced a unique design, known as the 'inclined action', which slopes downwards at the bass end of the keyboard – in order to maintain the correct hammer strike position on the radically repositioned bass strings (see the photograph on page 34). A full list of Jack Davis's designs – grands, uprights or minis – is shown in appendix 4.

His most successful model, from a tonal point of view, is the instrument called *Miniroyal*, which was introduced in 1958. Known within the factory as the 'model 90', it has a strikingly original case (designed by a certain Mr Hadden) in which the top and top door are 'welded' together as one piece, to form a kind of 'bonnet'. It also has an attractive grand-piano-style music rest. The case is without columns or extending toes, and the keyboard is supported at each end by a pair of simple 'cheeks' which jut out into mid-air at the front of the instrument. A unique feature of this particular case design is the way in which the keyboard fall can be usefully secreted away, inside the piano, and conveniently out of the way of the pianist's playing hands. This latter design feature was invented by Gerald Brasted, one of the sons of Percy, and was patented.[12] The piano's novel casework was very popular with the dealers, and the instrument sold well in music shops. The quality of its bass tone is surprisingly good, considering the small size of the instrument, and certainly contributed towards successful sales of the model.

Post War production

Harry Brasted, the eldest of the four brothers, died in February 1950, and his younger brother, Percy, followed in October 1954. The Eavestaff firm was now taken over by a new generation of the family: the brothers Douglas, Gerald and Frederick (sons of Percy Brasted) and their cousin Clifford (son of Albert Brasted). An outline tree of the Brasted family appears in appendix 3. From the mid-1930s, the Eavestaff company had cornered the market for the very small upright: there was almost no competition. From the early 1950s, however, practically every other British firm of piano maker went out of its way to build some kind of diminutive upright model. The Kemble *Minx* was perhaps the most well-known of these. Other versions of six-octave 'miniatures' made by the firms of Zender, Barratt & Robinson or Bentley, seriously undercut Eavestaff in price; and a small Monington & Weston model appears to have been a blatant carbon copy of the Eavestaff *Miniroyal's* case design. It is an old adage which states that it is 'the destiny of every pioneer to be superseded'. Brasted was certainly a piano pioneer during the 1930s, but was increasingly being overtaken by other manufacturers as the 1950s and '60s progressed.

Those decades witnessed a slow but steady decline in numbers of Eavestaff minis and other types of piano being produced at Hermitage Road. 1955 was a very good year for the company, during which a staggering 220 models per week appear to have left the factory. But this level of output was never attained again. During the following year, 1956, output dropped dramatically to around 100 per week, with a further decline to no more than 70 in 1957. From 1963, the company never produced more than 30 in any one

The upper photo shows the interior of the Eavestaff 'Miniroyal' with inclined action. The lower photo shows the rear of the piano, with diagonally-grained soundboard and diagonal ribbing. Designed by Jack Davis, 1958. The piano illustrated here is probably the prototype.

[Photo: Author's collection]

The Eavestaff 'Miniroyal', model 90, with casework designed by Hadden.
[Illustration from an Eavestaff publicity brochure, c.1965]

week; and by the year 1968, an average of only ten Eavestaff models left the Harringay works on a weekly basis.[13]

An event which happened around the year 1960 further helps to explain this steady decline in Eavestaff output: Brasted Brothers Ltd purchased the Challen company, and commenced the manufacture of new Challen grand and upright instruments at Hermitage Road, alongside the usual Eavestaff production. Although the output of Challen models shrank more or less in line with Eavestaff's from 1960, the numbers of Challen pianos made actually began to exceed those minis bearing the Eavestaff name. For example, in 1968, approximately fifteen Challens left Hermitage Road each week, but only around ten Eavestaffs. This phenomenon suggests that the larger Challen uprights must have been selling better than the smaller Eavestaff equivalents; the piano-buying public appeared to be on the point of a fashionable return to the merits of the larger upright. In fact, from the late 1960s, larger, traditional-looking uprights began to be imported from Japan by Yamaha and Kawai, and the musical public began to appreciate once more the joys of playing an upright piano of musically appropriate dimensions. Brasted never made any attempt to launch a big, bold model to compete with this new Japanese influx, but persevered with its customary diminutive versions.

The Eavestaff 'Minitronic' electro-acoustic keyboard, c.1970.
[Illustration from an Eavestaff publicity brochure, c.1970]

The Minitronic

A very tragic episode marked the closing months at Hermitage Road during the late 1960s: there had been costly and time-consuming research involved in the development of a completely new kind of instrument, a small electro-acoustic keyboard known as the *Minitronic*. This tiny, box-like instrument (115cm by 59cm) was visually very much like the small, transistorised electronic organs of the day. It was mounted on four legs, and had hand controls to adjust volume and tone quality. Although this instrument marked a completely new departure for Brasted, it was seen as the natural and logical successor to the 'acoustic' mini. There was a growing understanding in the Trade that the traditional piano was inevitably entering an unfamiliar electronic world. At its launch, the *Minitronic* received very good press, and was highly commended for its innovative details, such as its light aluminium frame which supported the horizontal stringing load. The instrument had one string for each note. Its best feature was its 'touch sensitive' action, which had been designed in-house by Jack Davis, cleverly utilising existing upright piano action components. It was an action superior to many of those found in electric pianos of a later date.

Unfortunately, the Minitronic design had two fatal flaws: it was strung at very low tension with very delicate, thin steel wires, and did not stay in tune at all well; and secondly, within months of the launch of the model, Brasted's postbox was full of letters from frustrated customers demanding replacements for those strings which had suddenly snapped. For these reasons, the model was quickly withdrawn from production, and Brasted must have suffered serious financial consequences as a result. Jack Davis was to spend the rest of his life engaged in the tedious chore of sending out replacement strings. Between 1973 and 1976, for example, he was obliged to send out three hundred of them to dis-satisfied customers.[14]

The closure of Hermitage Road

It came as something of a shock when the Hermitage Road factory suddenly closed in the spring of 1970, and the workforce was laid off. The closure marked the sad end to a long and highly successful period of piano making on the site. Over a span of thirty-five years, something like 20,000 instruments, mainly minis, had been born under the roof of the factory. The little musical creations were to be found all over the world, bringing an inestimable amount of pleasure to their numerous owners, and fame to the Eavestaff name. The goodwill attached to the trademark *Eavestaff* survived the closure, but it was sold on to others, who chose to have instruments with the name attached made in the Far East.[15] Perhaps the greatest tragedy of all surrounding the Brasted closure is this: never again in this country could a workforce of the kind seen at Hermitage Road be assembled with sufficient skills to embark upon the manufacture of pianos: the skills simply do not exist anymore in this country; and the way in which so-called 'market forces' have casually allowed manual skills in Britain to perish over the past few decades is nothing short of a national disgrace.

Brasted Brothers Ltd could have had the option of down-sizing, and could have opened a new plant focused on the production of far fewer pianos but of higher quality, perhaps with an output of no more than five per week. There were a few old-established London companies, such as Chappell, Broadwood and Monington & Weston, who were making pianos on this basis in 1970, as well as the growing number of harpsichord makers, who were content to craft no more than one or two instruments per month. But Brasted Brothers Ltd were, more than anything else, 'volume producers', and it is very hard to imagine the company being satisfied with such a modest arrangement. 'Pianos are like prams' announced Percy Brasted on one occasion. 'If you push them, they will go.'[16] This statement perhaps sums up the Brasted brothers' unsentimental attitude towards the piano: it was essentially another commercial commodity which, if made in sufficient quantities and marketed in the right way, would achieve a handsome profit for everyone concerned.

3
THE SQUIRE FAMILY OF PIANOMAKERS

THE surname 'Squire' occurs over and over again in the surviving records of London piano making covering the period roughly between 1830 to 1970. We are intrigued to know whether all the individuals involved and surnamed Squire were in fact part and parcel of the same family. Although the majority of Squires were never regarded as 'major' manufacturers (as far as their quantity of output is concerned), it would be correct to suggest that they very much represented the 'backbone' of London-based piano-making, and served the Trade in many differing ways: as designers, makers, tuners, dealers and repairers. We can count up an impressive number of at least twenty-two family members of the 'Squirearchy' attached to the industry; and, yes, they were indeed all related.

In this chapter, we shall follow the careers of those members of the family for whom pianos became an important part of their working lives. Each member named in the account has been given their own individual number, so as to help avoid the inevitable confusion which arises when attempting to distinguish one from another. There is also a family 'tree' which appears in appendix 5, showing most of the piano-making family members, and which aids further clarification. Some of the Squires were highly successful, and lived comfortably from the financial profits resulting from their endeavours; others were careless and even reckless with money (and this seems to have been an unfortunate family trait), and we come across a fair share of bankruptcies and business failures – which also goes to show how precarious the Piano Trade could be in the period under examination.

As far as we can ascertain, the vast majority of family members involved in the Trade were involved in a very *practical* 'hands on' way: they did not regard themselves simply as office administrators. There was a continuity of high skill level running through the family, which was treasured; and even the most successful of them, Frank Squire of B. Squire & Son, with his huge factory in Stanhope Street, Euston Road, preferred to spend his days on the shop floor supervising production and checking over instruments – toning and regulating them before their final despatch – rather than sitting in an office. He was also preoccupied with an adequate training of vital manual skills for his apprentices.

1: William Brinsmead Squire (c.1808-1864)

The first thing we know about the family is that its piano-making members originated from north Devon: the two earliest-known were William Brinsmead Squire (born c.1808 at St Giles in the Wood, near Bideford) and John Squire (born c.1812 at Great Torrington, also near Bideford). We can guess that the two were related in some way or other, although their precise connection has yet to be established.

William was the son of a certain Esther Squire (born 1781), an unmarried woman. His middle name, Brinsmead, is the strong pointer to the likely surname of his father. In fact, at a later date William and his children appear to have been close friends with the famous piano maker John Brinsmead (1814-1908) who was a near contemporary of William, and who was also a Devonian, born at Wear Gifford.[1] The three villages of St Giles, Torrington and Wear Gifford lie within a few miles of each other.

By the year 1829, William had reached London, and on the 16th October of that year he married Betsy Chambers at St Pancras Old Church. She was also a Devonian, hailing from the town of Exeter. The official date of the establishment of William's business was also later given as 1829. The young couple were soon to produce a huge family of ten children. They first lived and worked in the St Pancras district of London, but by the early 1860s, William and Betsy were living at a fashionable and expensive address, at 27, Upper Montague Street, Marylebone. Of their large number of offspring, only *one* son, Frank, was to succeed to his father's business. We can identify at least one particular family trait from the mid-nineteenth century: the need of each of the sons, bar one, to be free from their father's control, and to carry on their own businesses independently. Perhaps William was a difficult and cantankerous individual to work with.

His piano making career had been financially successful: he left some £800 at the time of his death in January 1864, at the comparatively young age of fifty-six.[2] His widow Betsy was left to bring up the children, three of whom were not yet twenty-one at the time of her husband's death. William Brinsmead Squire's will is reproduced as appendix 6, from which it can readily be seen how the one son, Frank, was favoured above all the other brothers or sisters – which is likely to have led to a certain amount of jealousy coming from his siblings, and some resentfulness towards his father.

Nevertheless, we have the one endearing tale handed down about this first William Squire: high up on the flat roof of his piano factory, situated at 76, George Street, Euston Square, he took pains to construct a remarkable 'playground' area for his enormous family of ten children. Here, William and Betsy hoped, the young Squires would be out of harm's way – but they would no doubt be dragged down into the workshops below to help out with menial chores as and when things became busy![3]

2. John Squire (c.1812-1890)

The second individual in the Squire dynasty, John, was the sixth child of Henry and Grace Squire. When he first moved up to London, he lodged with Henry Brinsmead, John Brinsmead's older brother.[4] This is strong circumstantial evidence suggesting that John Squire, as well as William (1), was a kinsman of the Brinsmeads. Yet another London piano maker who originated from the same part of the country, George Youatt, is reputed to have been part of a group of young woodworkers who journeyed together from north Devon to London in search of work, sometime in the 1830s or early 1840s. Perhaps John Squire travelled up to London in the company of George Youatt?[5]

John and his wife Susan (nee Hancock) settled in London at a later date than William Squire. We know this because their eldest child, Henry, was in fact born in Devon, at Great Torrington in 1833, as was their third child, Thomas, born in the same place circa 1843. John will have first journeyed to London alone – he was certainly living there in 1841 – but he had left his wife and young family at Torrington for the time being. The 1851 London Census Return shows the whole family to be now settled in London, however, and John to be described as a 'piano maker'. He was working (or had recently worked) for Collard & Collard, and there survives one of his cottage upright models with the inscription *John Squire from Collard & Collard* attached to its nameboard.[6] Twenty years later, John had ceased piano making and, curiously, was now active as an organ builder; but his son Henry **(10)** remained attached to piano manufacture.

John's first wife was Susan Hancock, another Devonian from Great Torrington, and we wonder if she was by chance a relation of the well-known Devon and London family of organ builders, Crang Hancock. If so, this might help to explain why John Squire eventually switched to organ building. When he died at the aptly-named Devon Lodge, Wood Green (on the northern outskirts of London) in 1890, he left £2,098, and so his keyboard instrument making activities over the previous fifty years had certainly been very remunerative. This cannot be said of his son, Henry Squire (**10**, see on.)

3: Betsy Squire (c.1807-1888)
Following the early death of her husband William **(1)**, Betsy appears to have taken over the running of the well-established piano-manufacturing concern. The instruments made under her supervision were known as *B. Squire*, this being necessary to avoid confusion with other pianos being constructed at the same time, and independently, by her eldest son, also called William (see **4**). Eventually, she was joined in partnership by the favoured son Frank, so that her piano's nameboards were to become inscribed *B. Squire & Son*. It has often been assumed that the certain 'B. Squire' was a male individual, and so it comes as a complete surprise to some to discover that the business was in fact being run by a female! Betsy eventually retired to Margate, Kent, where she died on the 20th June 1888, aged about eighty-one. She had outlived her husband by twenty-four years.

4: William Henry Squire 'the younger' (c.1830-1894)
William was the eldest son of William Brinsmead Squire, and was usually described as 'William Squire the younger' to distinguish him from his father. He was born in London around the year 1830. He and his wife Sophia raised a family of five children, of whom two of the sons (see **11** and **12**) were to enter the piano industry.

In 1859, the younger William unfortunately became bankrupt. An entry in the *London Gazette* of the 21st January of that year, when Squire was applying for a Court Protection Order, was at pains to notify the public that:

William Henry Squire, commonly known as William Squire the younger, formerly of no.33 Arlington-street, and afterwards of no.6, Gloucester Place, Gloucester

Crescent, both in Camden Town, and while of both places having a workshop at No.1 Brook-street, Euston-road, St Pancras, and there carrying on business, as a Pianoforte Maker, then of No. 332 Euston-road aforesaid, Coffee and Eating House Keeper, during a portion of the time also residing at Gloucester-place aforesaid, and also during part of the same time a Pianoforte Maker, afterwards of no.12A and now of no.30, both in Victoria-road Kentish-town, all in Middlesex, Journeyman Pianoforte Maker.[7]

This evidence tells us that William was at least enterprising, if nothing else, somehow having the useful mix of a catering career intertwined with that of piano making. He must have recovered financially from his bankruptcy ordeal, because ten years later he was still in business, in partnership with his younger brother Alfred, trading as *Squire Brothers*, piano makers and music sellers, with premises at 157 Tottenham Court Road and 1A Beaumont Place, Euston Road. This partnership was wound up by mutual consent on the 22nd December 1869, leaving William Henry to carry on the business single-handed.[8] According to the London Census Return of 1891, William Henry Squire, now aged sixty, lived at 93, Camden Street, Camden Town and was still in business as a piano maker, but he was to die within four years.

5: Roland Montague Squire (1833-1922)

This individual with the rather exotic name was the second son of William Brinsmead Squire, and was born in London in 1833. He met a certain Adelaide, a music teacher from the city of Liverpool. By the year 1861 the couple had married and settled in Liverpool, where they lived in the district close to the present Anglican Cathedral. Roland had a most unfortunate business career, and suffered the same misfortune as his older brother; but in his case, he became bankrupt twice: in 1862 and 1873. In the bankruptcy proceedings of 1862, Roland was described as 'a Music and Musical Instrument Dealer, Tuner and Chapman'. In 1873, when he was again adjudged bankrupt, he was described as:

Roland Montague Squire, residing and carrying on business as a Pianoforte and Musical Instrument Maker, at No.45, Seymour Street, Liverpool in the county of Lancaster, and also carrying on business as a Licensed Victualler, at the Alexandra Theatre, Lime Street, Liverpool aforesaid.[9]

By the year 1881, Roland Montague had disappeared from English history: he had emigrated to Canada – perhaps to escape from his creditors. His wife Adelaide was no longer with him (she may have sadly died) and the 1881 Census Return for the St Lawrence Ward of Montreal city shows that he was living there with a certain Emma Squire, his second wife, and also with his son by his first wife, fifteen-year-old Roland Alfred. In spite of all his upheavals in life, Roland Montague was still, determinedly, making pianos.[10] He and his wife are buried in the Mount Royal Cemetery, Montreal.

6: Frank Squire (c.1836-1923) of B. Squire & Son

Of all the members of the Squire family engaged in the piano industry, Frank Squire appears to have been by far the most successful. He appears to have made many more pianos than any other Squire, and there is still a considerable number of *B. Squire & Son* instruments in circulation. As musical instruments, his uprights are of robust and conscientious construction, with a strong and sustained tone. (We have no evidence to show that he ever manufactured grands.) But in design, his uprights are very old-fashioned for their day. We can understand this in the light of the fact that Frank was over eighty years of age when many of his surviving instruments will have been constructed, and at that sort of age he was unlikely to have embraced change. It should be pointed out, however, that from the 1930s, the goodwill attached to the name 'B. Squire & Son' had been purchased by Kemble and Company, and later Kemble-built Squire instruments were quite different (and of more modern design) when compared with the original instruments built under Frank's supervision at the Stanhope Street factory.

Frank Squire was the one son entrusted by his father William (**1**) to continue the piano manufacturing business established in 1829, which he dutifully did, along with his mother Betsy, for many a year. The London Census Return of 1881 informs us that Frank was employing sixty-three men and nine apprentices at that date. Frank married twice, and eventually produced an enormous family of thirteen children by his two wives: six daughters and seven sons. We can imagine the sons – and later the grandsons – scurrying around helping at the Stanhope Street workshops, being supervised and dominated by the tyrannical patriarch. There is one rather unappealing legend which survives about Frank: it concerns his method of reprimanding his employees for not carrying out a job in a satisfactory manner:

Frank Squire (1836-1923).
[From The Pianomaker *magazine, April 1923]*

Frank, when passing through the various workshops of his factory, would carry around with him in his pocket a small silver hammer. He would then use this to strike any particular instrument on which the workmanship was not up to his required standard. This highly aggressive action must have been extremely disliked by the workforce, as it damaged their work with bruises and dints which they were obliged to rectify! Frank's silver hammer was certainly a primitive and brutal way of expressing dissatisfaction, but it appears to have maintained quality control.[11]

When Frank Squire died on the 11th April 1923 at the advanced age of about eighty-seven, he was an extremely wealthy man: according to his probate documentation, he left £26,973, a fortune at that date.[12] Nevertheless, the firm of B. Squire and Son had been making heavy losses for many years, and Frank must have been obliged to 'bale out' the company on a number of occasions from his own private means. Under the terms of his will, he bequeathed his 'leasehold premises number 3 Stanhope Street Euston Road together with the plant machinery fittings fixtures and trade utensils in and about the said premises and together also with the goodwill of my business of a Pianoforte Manufacturer carried on by me at the said premises' to two of his sons, Arthur William Squire (**14**) and Ernest Ebeneezer Squire (**15**). Following his death, his fortune was soon divided up, shared amongst his huge number of descendants. *The Pianomaker* magazine included the following interesting details about him in an obituary contained in its April 1923 issue:

> Frank Squire had a great struggle in building up the business, but in the early 'seventies' he had secured a factory output of about 1,000 pianos, a good total for those days, more particularly when it is borne in mind that every department came under his own supervision. He was as hard a worker as has ever been in the piano trade, he never shirked duty and he saw that others performed their work as they should. [Hence the silver hammer!] *In this respect he was a firm believer in the apprenticeship system, and in the second issue of 'The Pianomaker' there was a page article by him on this question, in which he claimed that the first essential of a skilled mechanic was the knowledge to handle tools properly. All his sons were put to the bench, and they were treated just as the other apprentices.*[13]

In many respects, Frank Squire shared the same personality traits as his kinsman, the famous London piano maker John Brinsmead. (There was a distinct physical resemblance as well!) Perhaps Brinsmead, with his enormous personal business success in the nineteenth century, provided Frank Squire with some kind of role model?

7: Alfred 'Taff' Squire (c.1840-1925)

Compared with his older brother Frank, Alfred 'Taff' Squire was relatively impoverished at the time of his death in 1925, leaving only £223. And yet he was certainly the most interesting Squire of his generation. He had wide experience in the industry, a versatile range of skills, and he was a creative, inventive and scholarly personality. He served the Trade as an accomplished freelance 'scale designer' for many a year. There were few London manufacturers who had not benefited, in one way or another, from his scale-design skills. In his old age, Alfred boasted that he was 'The Architect of the Industry'. The justification for his claim will shortly be explained.

In his youth, Alfred was known to have been on very friendly terms with the piano maker, John Brinsmead. This is not surprising really, considering that the Squires and the Brinsmeads were somehow related. It was in all probability this particular family connection which helped to lead to Alfred Squire's appointment as manager at the Kentish Town factory of the firm of John Brinsmead and Sons. This was a highly responsible position, given that he is likely to have been in charge of over one hundred workmen. We can only guess as to the date when this appointment commenced. It might have been in the 1870s, when Alfred was in his thirties.

It is highly likely that it was during his period with Brinsmead that he was able to begin to develop and hone his skills as a piano scale designer. Whilst working in the factory, he would have had ample opportunity to study the intricacies of such things as stringing layout, string tensions, wire gauges, hammer strike points, down-bearing pressures and cast-iron frame structural design. He may even have participated in the design of a number of new Brinsmead models, but unfortunately we have no evidence to confirm or deny this possibility. On leaving his employment with Brinsmead, probably sometime in the 1880s, Alfred took an unusual step: he negotiated with a Scottish firm of piano frame iron-founders named Smith & Wellstood of Bonnybridge, Stirlingshire, to become their agent in London. The firm's main business had once been the casting of sewing machine bodies for the American Singer company; but after Singer began to make its own castings at Clydebank from 1882, the Bonnybridge company urgently needed to turn to other sources of work, and a new line was developed to provide finished cast-iron frames (fettled, drilled, pinned and japanned) for the London-based piano trade.[14]

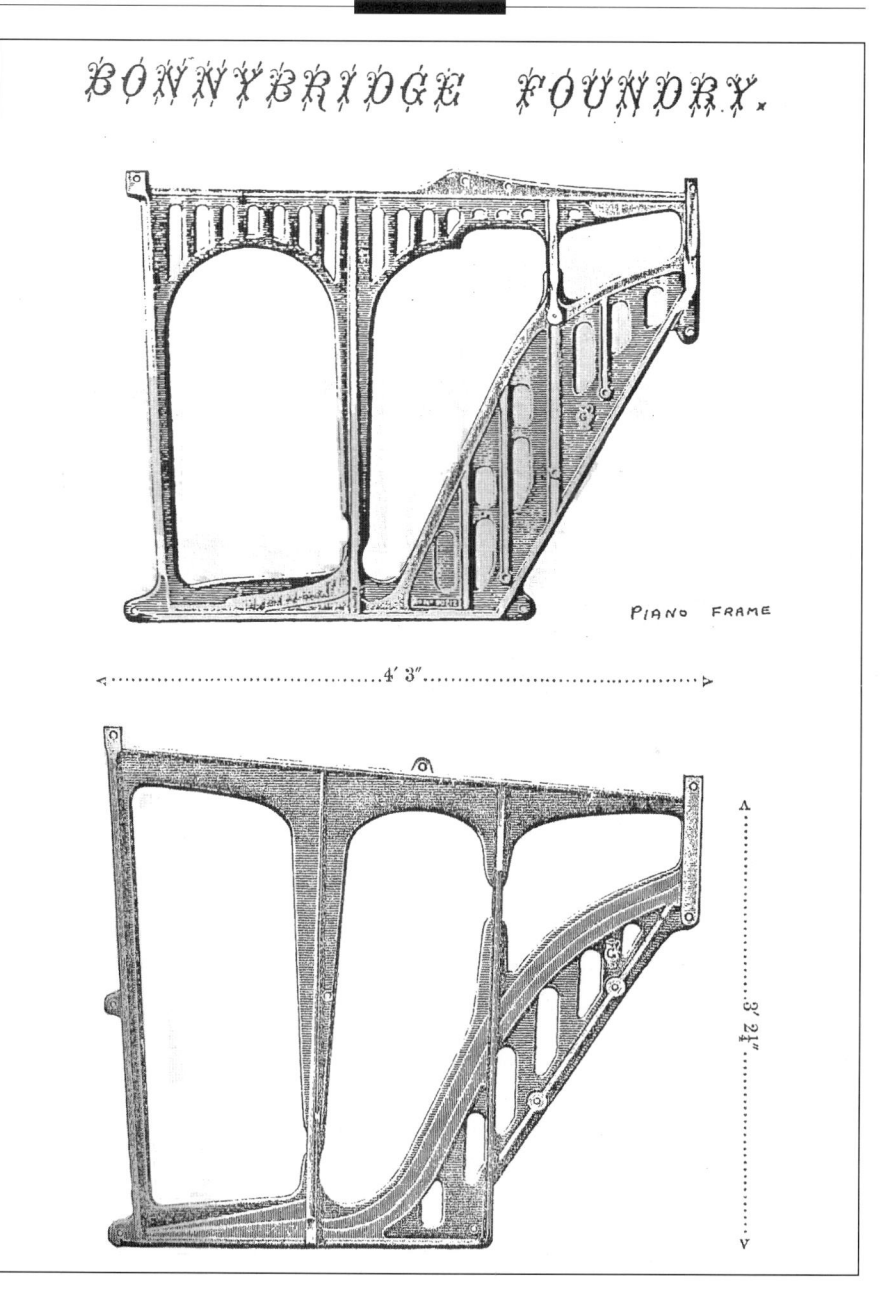

Two cast-iron upright piano frames from Smith & Wellstood's ironfoundry, c.1885, probably designed by Alfred Squire.
[Smith & Wellstood ironfoundry records, Falkland Council Archives, Falkirk, Scotland]

Alfred Squire was not just a 'sales representative' for Smith & Wellstood: he became involved in an interesting scheme linking the Scottish iron-founders with the numerous London piano makers: he provided a kind of 'service' which enabled aspiring piano makers to speedily and economically go into production. He would design an instrument, personally make all necessary manufacturing jigs and templates, and then sell these on to a particular piano manufacturer as requested. Then he would send off his drawing, together with the necessary wooden foundry pattern, to Smith & Wellstood. Within a matter of a few weeks, the Scottish foundry would have a batch of finished frames ready, made to Alfred's design, for sale directly to the piano manufacturer in question – and for immediate installation into instruments in the course of construction. This particular 'service' must have been very attractive to the smaller makers with their limited knowledge of piano design, or with limited capital to research and develop their own models. Alfred Squire was the highly-useful 'go between' who enabled things to happen. Smith & Wellstood would benefit from increased sales; and the various London piano manufacturers would doubtless have been grateful for the input of Alfred's unique expertise.

Piano frames made under this arrangement were known as 'standard frames', because the same 'standard' scale design (particularly a successful one) might have been utilised on the frames supplied to a number of different makers. Not only was the general public unaware of this customary practice: the piano makers themselves would have little knowledge as to who was using which particular standard scale at any one time. A surviving order book from the Smith & Wellstood Archive, spanning the period circa 1890 to circa 1915, shows that almost every London piano manufacturer was dealing with the Scottish foundry[15] (although the Scottish company was certainly not the only supplier of cast frames at that time). The order book certainly gives us some insight into the likely extent of Alfred Squire's role in making new designs readily available for a multitude of makers.

We cannot understand how Alfred earned the nickname 'Taff', especially as his regular business connections were Scottish ones rather than Welsh! Louis Bamberger, in his publication *Memories of Sixty Years in the Timber and Pianoforte Trades* (circa 1930) provided a final brief anecdote:

> I was not aware that 'Taff' had passed away a couple of years ago. At one time he was almost indispensable to many piano firms in the production of scales. In his later days he was afflicted with deafness and other infirmities, but in the heyday of his strength 'Taff' derived a good income from the trade. I believe he claimed to be the 'architect' of the industry.

In his will dated the 29th April 1922, Alfred Squire bequeathed to his eldest son Wallace William Collard Squire (**16**) his 'lathe and all the tools in my workshop including bench and work table also all pianoforte scales and wood patterns now at Messrs Smith and Wellstood, Bonnybridge, Stirlingshire, Scotland.'

8: Albert Alexander Squire (1842-1908) co-founder of 'Squire & Longson'

Albert was the seventh son of William and Betsy (**1**) and (**3**). He had married a French woman, Henrietta Horrenburger, a teacher of music from Paris. He was appointed administrator of his mother Betsy's estate after her death in 1888. We know nothing about his early career in the industry, but he is remembered as being the co-founder, with John H. Longson, of the firm of piano makers *Squire & Longson*, in the year 1883. The firm was first established at Arlington Road, Camden Town, but moved around the year 1891 to number 40, Great College Street, also in Camden Town. The partnership soon earned a reputation as the makers of good quality instruments, available at a reasonable price.

The tie-up with Longson is curious, because John H. Longson was actually a professional violin maker and not at all involved with pianos until he joined up with Albert Squire. Some of his instruments still survive, and are known to the violin-making fraternity. (There appear to be no other recorded instances of a professional violin maker having had such a notable change of career!) Born in 1849, Longson was a Lancashire man, who must have moved to London and taken the bold decision to abandon violins in favour of pianos. He must have noted that the financial remuneration derived from piano manufacturing could be far greater than that of a solitary violin maker!

As well as making pianos under their own name, the Squire & Longson partnership used the trademark *Cremona*. This may be found on the iron frame castings of some of their instruments dating from 1904.[16] The choice of name was no doubt John Longson's, as he would have known and admired the many excellent violins emanating from the Italian city of Cremona. Following the death of Albert (or A.A. Squire as he was usually known) in 1908, the firm continued to be run by John Longson, aided by his former partner's son, Charles Albert Squire (**18**). Longson became ill in the autumn of 1915, resigned his position with the company, and moved back north to Blackburn, Lancashire, leaving Charles Squire in sole charge of the business. He was to die in Lancashire on the 12th March 1916.[17]

9: Byron Squire (c. 1847-1915)
This individual with the poetic first name was the eighth son of William and Betsy Squire. Our earliest records about him indicate that he was in partnership with his older brother Frank (**6**); but an announcement in the *London Gazette* of the 22nd May 1877 notified the public that the partnership had been wound up. Frank continued to trade from 3 & 5 Stanhope Street, Euston Road, as *B. Squire & Son*, whereas thirty-year old Byron's separate business was styled, for some unknown reason, as *Croft & Son*. But Byron was soon to leave England: there is no trace of him in the London Census Return of 1881: he had emigrated to Auckland, New Zealand, where he opened a piano and music business. It is highly likely that he will have imported London-built Squire pianos, constructed in the workshops of one or other of his brothers.[18]

The biographies of the sons of William Brinsmead Squire and his wife Betsy end here, and we now turn to the offspring of William's contemporary from Devon, John Squire:

10: Henry Squire of Islington (1833-1906)
Henry was the son of John and Susan Squire (**2**), and was born at Great Torrington, Devon, in 1833, before his parents had left for the capital. Like many of the Squires, he appears to have had no wish to remain attached to his father's business: at the young age of about twenty-three, he had managed to establish his own piano-building firm in a substantial factory at number 25, Hollingsworth Street, Liverpool Road, Islington, London. He clearly had great ambition; but he suffered a terrible blow as a result of an event which was reported in *Lloyd's Weekly Newspaper* of August 8th 1858:

> *On Friday morning a fire, involving the destruction of a large amount of property, broke out in the extensive premises of Mr Henry Squire, pianoforte manufacturer, No. 25, Hollingsworth-street, Liverpool-road, Holloway.*
>
> *The discovery was made by some of the neighbours, who aroused the inmates and despatched the police for the society's fire escapes, which were promptly on the spot, under the direction of Inspector Baddeley, and rendered most essential service on the occasion. The brigade engines from Watling-street, Farringdon-street, Jeffrey-square, Holborn, and the two powerful parish engines from Islington followed very quickly. As is too frequently the case, there was at first a scarcity of water, and the most strenuous exertions of all present failed to make the slightest impression on the flames,*

which ignited the dwelling house, which also fell a prey to the flames. A plentiful supply being now obtained, the engines were got to work in admirable manner, but notwithstanding great exertions, the manufactory and dwelling, with their valuable contents, were burnt out, and the adjoining houses considerably damaged. The cause of the outbreak is unknown. The loss will fall on the Phoenix and other offices.[19]

Although Henry must have been insured, he appears to have lost his family home adjoining the factory, as well as the factory itself. According to an announcement nine years later, in the *London Gazette* of the 5th April 1867, his chronic financial troubles had led him to be thrown into the Debtors Prison for London and Middlesex.[20] We cannot prove that the earlier tragic fire of 1858 was one of the underlying causes of Henry's problems, but it seems highly likely. Perhaps he had been insufficiently insured to cover his enormous losses?

Poor Henry appears to have remained in the Debtors Prison for three months, during which time a petition of bankruptcy was filed against him. Somehow, thankfully, the funds to repay his creditors were eventually found, and on the 19th July 1867, he was granted Discharge from his bankruptcy.[21] We can guess that his father John, and other piano-making relatives, might have got together in order to save him. Undeterred by his terrible misfortunes, Henry plunged into piano manufacture once again: by 1881, he was in business at Campbell Road, Islington.

He must have been joined by his eldest son, Charles, born around the year 1852. Although Charles and his nineteen-year-old wife Georgina appear in the 1871 Finsbury Census Return (in which he is described as a 'piano maker'), we can find no trace of the couple after this date. Perhaps they chose to emigrate? By the year 1901, Henry Squire, now aged sixty-eight, had given up piano work. He is described in the Census Return of that year as a 'retired piano maker' and lived at 32, Umfreyville Road, Hornsey. He was to die five years later, in January 1906, with no obvious successors; and yet a piano manufacturing company named as *Henry Squire & Company*, and trading from Wrotham Piano Works, 1a, Elm Road, Camden Town, was advertising in the August and December 1920 issues of *The Pianomaker* magazine. Unfortunately, we have no way at present of linking this later firm with the earlier one established by Henry back in the 1850s.

Here ends our account of the contribution of John Squire's dynasty to the piano industry. We now turn to the grand-children of William and Betsy Squire:

11 and 12: William Henry Squire junior and Frederick Roland Squire
These two brothers, the sons of William Henry Squire (4) were in business together, probably in a small way, at Bayham Place, Camden Town, from around the year 1885. Frederick broke away from the partnership in 1905, and started his own firm in Harmood Street, Camden Town. This enterprise survived until 1917, when Frederick sold out to the Harper Piano Company. His older brother William Henry moved his business to the Stoke Newington district of London – to 16a Albion Road. He lost two of his piano-making sons during World War I (William and Arthur) but in 1919 was joined by his only-surviving son, Herbert (born 1895). In the June 1919 edition of *The Pianomaker* magazine, William determinedly announced: *In the next thirty-five years my son and myself want to make 6 pianos per working day*. He must have been a highly-optimistic individual, and one anxious to overcome the set-backs his family had recently endured as a result of the War. Nevertheless, the name William Squire slowly disappears from the industry during the 1920s. If the firm did indeed survive, then its output must have been very modest.

13: Francis Henry Squire (1862-1928) of H. Hicks & Son
The eldest son of Frank Squire of *B. Squire & Son*, Francis Henry, was trained in his father's factory in Stanhope Street, Euston Road, and was no doubt

Francis Henry Squire with his wife Minnie (seated). Standing behind, their three sons: left to right: Franz, Frederick and Leonard. Photo taken 1912.
[Photo: Frank Squire family archive]

being groomed to eventually become the leading light in the family concern. He must have had a wide range of piano-making skills. Sadly, Francis Henry developed a serious gambling habit, which also involved other employees of B. Squire & Son. According to his descendant, his disastrous losses as a result of unsuccessful gambling meant that he had to forfeit two of his homes in succession, and was eventually obliged to move into rented accommodation.[22] As circumstances worsened, Francis had the humiliation of being sacked by his father, and tragically, was denied the right to inherit his father's business. Whenever this was, it must have been a very harrowing time for the family. Nevertheless, because of his expert abilities as a piano maker, Francis Henry soon found employment elsewhere, and was appointed factory manager of the sizeable south London firm of piano makers, *H. Hicks & Son* of Newington Butts. By the mid-1920s, however, he had left Hicks, and became associated with a business known as *Squire Brothers*, established by two of his sons Franz Joseph (**18**) and Frederick Harold (**19**) at Hornsey, north London (see page 54). He died in early 1928.

14 and 15: Arthur William Squire (born c. 1871) and Ernest Ebeneezer Squire (c. 1875-1955)
These two brothers were the younger sons of Frank Squire of B. Squire & Son. They were bequeathed the piano-making business in Stanhope Street under the terms of their father's will; but from as early as 1908, Ernest Ebeneezer (**15**) appears to have gone his own way and had opened up a piano and music shop at New Broadway, Ealing, west London – later known as *Squires of Ealing*. He was financially very successful in this enterprise, and was succeeded at the shop by his son Roy Hughes Squire (**22**).

The elder of the two brothers, Arthur William (**14**), remained with the old established family business in Stanhope Street – he succeeded his father Frank after the latter's death in 1923. Following a re-organisation of the business in the summer of 1925, turning it into a limited company, Arthur remained as factory manager; but just over one year later, in September 1926, he decided to sell his shares in B. Squire & Son, and resigned his post.[23] Things did not appear to be working out well for him by this date; he clearly wished to distance himself from the business. *His* son, Wallace Gordon Squire (c.1893-1976) wanted to be a farmer's boy, and this he had succeeded in doing by 1911, when he was living on a farm in Bedfordshire as an agricultural apprentice. Clearly, pianos were of no interest to him! The Stanhope Street factory of B. Squire & Son was eventually to close in 1929, exactly one hundred years after the original manufacturing business had been founded.

16 and 17: Wallace William Collard Squire and Leopold Alfred Squire (died 1948)

Wallace and Leopold were the sons of Alfred 'Taff' Squire (**7**) and they were both involved in the piano industry. As we have seen, under the terms of Alfred's will, his 'pianoforte scales and wooden patterns' were bequeathed to his eldest son, Wallace. From this fragment of information, we can suggest that Wallace might have continued where his father had left off: as a piano scale designer to the industry. The amount of work for such an occupation, however, was certainly drying up as the 1920s progressed, with more and more piano factories closing down. Leopold, Wallace's younger brother, moved into piano retailing: he eventually became the proprietor of a long-established provincial piano and music shop, *James Dace and Son* of Chelmsford, Essex.

18: Charles Albert Squire (born c. 1874)

Charles was the only son of Albert A. Squire (see number (**8**), co-founder of Squire & Longson. Following the death of his father's partner John H. Longson in 1916, Charles appears to have been running the piano-making firm single-handedly for a few years. At the end of the First War, however, he closed down his own factory in Camden Town, and, joining in partnership with a certain Clarence Lyon, moved his business south of the River, where a new company run by Lyon and Squire, known as *Cremona Ltd*, began trading from Medlar Street, Camberwell. (It will be remembered that the trade mark 'Cremona' had in fact been first used by Squire & Longson as early as 1904.)

Throughout the 1920s, the firm produced a range of 'trade' pianos, to which a variety of names might have been attached: as well as the name *Squire & Longson*, Cremona Ltd also manufactured pianos bearing the marques *Ronson*, *Paul Newman* and *Welmar*. For a highly-detailed account of Cremona Ltd's activities during the 1920s and early '30s, the reader is referred to chapter 5 (pages 94-113) of the author's publication, *Five London Piano Makers* (2010).

We now turn to the fourth generation of Squire piano makers:

19, 20 and 21: Franz Joseph Wallace Squire (1896-1970), Frederick Harold Squire (1898-1984), and Leonard William Squire (1900-1978)

These three brothers were the sons of Francis Henry Squire (**13**) of *B. Squire & Son* and *H. Hicks & Son*. They served their apprenticeships at their grandfather Frank Squire's factory in Stanhope Street, their particular knowledge being in the making of upright piano 'backs'. In May 1921, by now free of their grandfather's business, the two elder brothers commenced trading in equal partnership as specialist strung back manufacturers, under the name *Squire Brothers*. Their workshops were in Mortimer's Yard, Wightman Road, Hornsey, north London. A piano 'strung back' is an important component of every upright piano: it comprises the wooden back bracings behind the soundboard, the soundboard itself with its pinned bridges attached, the cast-iron frame (also attached) and finally the numerous strings and tuning pins, which are fitted towards the end of the assembly process. The arrival of a 'strung back' at one of the smaller piano manufacturers would have been a welcome sight: it would have saved a great deal of manufacturing time and space, and would have enabled that manufacturer to proceed rapidly towards the assembly of outer casework and the installation of the mechanical action and keys.

By 1927, the brothers' partnership was in serious financial trouble. Frederick withdrew from the business on the 1st March of that year, leaving Franz to struggle on alone, helped for a short time by his father, Francis Henry (**13**), who died in early 1928. In the following September, Franz Squire was declared bankrupt, with debts amounting to £377 9s 5d. (which were certainly extremely modest when compared with the £44,000 worth of debts owed by the insolvent J. & J. Hopkinson four years earlier. See chapter 4). At the bankruptcy proceedings, Franz attributed his failure to 'lack of capital, depression in trade, and to the profits of the business being insufficient to meet his drawing there from'.[24]

Following his brother's unfortunate bankruptcy, Frederick Harold Squire (**20**) had had enough of the piano trade, and started a new (and successful) career in insurance. (His two specialist 'bow drills', together with the bow, used for the drilling of a multitude of small holes in piano bridges before the guide pins are inserted, were donated to the writer of this book by Frank Squire, Frederick's nephew.)[25] The youngest of the three brothers, Leonard William (**21**), was the only one of his generation to continue in a practical capacity within the piano industry: between 1945 and 1960 he was employed at the well-known manufacturers, Charles H. Challen of Harringay, where his piano back-making skills would have been utilised and appreciated.[26]

22: Roy Hughes Squire (1909-1989)

As far as we know, this individual was the very last member of the Squirearchy to be actively involved in the piano trade. In 1955, he succeeded his father Ernest (**15**) in the piano and music retailing business known as *Squires of Ealing*, and continued working at the retail shop until his retirement.

THE 3' 6" SLIM-LINE MODEL
O/strung U/damper in Solid Mahogany.

An upright piano in solid mahogany, bearing the name William Squire, *displayed at the Earl's Court Radio, Television and Piano Exhibition, August 1961. Although it bears the 'Squire' name, the instrument's actual manufacturer is, surprisingly, unknown.*

[Author's collection]

4
ROGERS & HOPKINSON

THESE two well-known London makes were interlinked from the spring of 1924. In fact, from this date onwards, the Rogers piano as a musical instrument was indistinguishable from the Hopkinson: the two shared exactly the same internal designs and internal constructional features. Only slight stylistic differences to their external casework distinguished one brand from the other. As the road to the two firms' eventual tie-up is quite complicated, the author of this book feels it best to clarify things (before plunging into a detailed account of their respective histories) by providing an outline as to how the two companies eventually became one.

Around the year 1913, the Rogers company did not appear to have any family successors, following the retirement of the brothers Tom and Charles Rogers; and so the old-established business was sold to a certain Dr Charles Vincent, who appears to have been an accomplished businessman, with a surprising degree of financial clout at his fingertips. Then in April 1919, the surviving members of the piano-making Hopkinson family, also having no younger members with an interest in piano making, sold out their equally long-established concern to a consortium comprised of the Hermitage brothers and Frank Challen, the latter having been Hopkinson's factory manager for some fifteen years. Challen sadly died three months later, and then within five years the Hermitages had sadly brought the business into financial ruin through excessive discounting. Hopkinson was placed into receivership in January 1924. This date marked the end of the independent company.

In March 1924, Dr Vincent's Rogers company was able to take over the defunct Hopkinson, and decided to move its own piano production into Hopkinson's commodious factory in Fitzroy Road, Primrose Hill, north London. Almost identical Hopkinson and Rogers models then began to be constructed under the same roof. From this date onwards, the two names became inseparable, despite changes in overall ownership on at least six occasions during the eighty years since then. Having sorted out the precise connection between the two firms, we can now proceed to examine the history and development of each of the two concerns.

The Hopkinsons at Leeds

The Hopkinson family had become settled and well established in the Yorkshire city of Leeds as early as the mid-seventeenth century.[1] A certain John Hopkinson, described in the Leeds Directories as a 'music master', can be traced in the city back to the year 1817, when he and his family lived in a very fashionable part of town, at 14, Queen's Square, on the northern fringes of what was becoming a rapidly burgeoning industrial metropolis. The earliest records about them indicate that they were involved in music teaching and music retailing, rather than piano making.[2] In this respect, they were very similar to Chappell & Company and J.B. Cramer & Company of London, both of whose music publishing and selling activities were established long before they gave any consideration to piano manufacture.

The Hopkinson's home and original business premises at 14, Queen's Square nevertheless features an extremely wide front doorway (that is, if number 14 has the same numbering today as it did in the 1820s), suggesting that this might have been specially made to ease the entry and exit of pianos of various kinds. By the year 1830, John Hopkinson had died, and the head of the household had become his widow, Elizabeth, living in Queen's Square with her young family. The Leeds Census Return for 1841 shows that her children comprised four individuals: a daughter Jane who was described on the Return as a 'music teacher', and three sons, John, James and Thomas Barker Hopkinson, who were all described in the same Census as 'music sellers'. Of these brothers, we believe that the eldest, John, was a violinist rather than a keyboard player.[3] (An outline tree of the Hopkinson family appears in appendix 7.)

The 'official' date of the establishment of their music-selling enterprise was the year 1835, when John the eldest son would have been around the age of twenty-four. All members of the family appear to have been musicians of one kind or another. In the years 1842 and 1847, for example, the brothers John and James Hopkinson were described in the local directories as 'music professors, publishers and sellers', with new retail premises at 6, Commercial Street, a busy shopping thoroughfare in the centre of Leeds.

Although the Hopkinsons were not yet piano makers, piano manufacture was nevertheless carried out in the city of Leeds during the opening decades of the nineteenth century. The Kirk family of cabinet makers, joiners and publicans, who lived a few streets away from the Hopkinsons, in the Woodhouse district of Leeds, were making pianos by the 1830s. One of their number, Wheatley Kirk, the licensee of the *Harrison's Arms*, patented a new design of cottage upright piano in 1836, which featured a quite radical and advanced design of iron frame to support the stringing load.[4] It is quite likely that the Hopkinsons sold Wheatley Kirk's instruments in their Commercial Street shop; and it is equally likely that a certain Edward Barker Gowland (born c.1821), a relative of Mrs Elizabeth Hopkinson (he also shared the same middle name as Thomas Barker Hopkinson), was living in Leeds and was probably working for Kirk in a practical way at the bench.

Mid-nineteenth century oil portraits of two members of the Hopkinson piano-making family, believed to be those of the original partners, the brothers John and James.
[Charles and Caroline Hopkinson family archive]

We can only guess as to the reasons for the senior partner John Hopkinson's decision to move to London and open an outlet for the Leeds firm in the capital. It is likely to have been a matter of sheer ambition, and the strong desire to expand the already successful business in Leeds. On the other hand, it is clear that John was anxious to become a piano manufacturer, and he might have been handicapped in Leeds, with its limited supply of specialised skilled workers, in particular those with knowledge of grand piano construction. He left for the capital in the year 1846, taking with him Edward Barker Gowland.

We can gain a good impression of the spectacular growth and development of the Hopkinson London business during the twenty year period, 1846-1866, by glancing through the following list:

1846: John Hopkinson moved to London, where he was soon employing six workmen and two apprentices in small workshop premises.[5] Edward Gowland became his workshop foreman. John's younger brother James remained in Leeds to manage the business there.
1851: John Hopkinson registered a patent for a new kind of grand piano action. In the same year, at the Great Exhibition in London, he displayed a grand having this new action, for which he was awarded a Prize Medal, and which helped to achieve fame for this product. By this date, the firm was known as *J. & J. Hopkinson*.
1851: the London Census Return of that year noted that John Hopkinson was employing 'about 47 men' in piano manufacture.
1853: New workshops were built in Diana Place, Euston Road, adjoining Gray and Davidson's organ-building factory. The premises were unfortunately destroyed by fire three years later.
1856: James Hopkinson joined his older brother in London. The youngest of the three brothers, Thomas, remained in Leeds, to take charge of the family's music selling activities there.
1861: The London Census Return of that year noted that James Hopkinson was now employing 103 men and 32 boys.
1866: A completely new factory was erected in Fitzroy Road, Primrose Hill, Camden Town, which in size approached similar factories in the same district of London occupied by the Collard, Chappell and Brinsmead companies.

The Great Exhibition of 1851
It was the Hopkinson's display of a solitary instrument at the Great Exhibition which was of enormous help in making the piano-buying public

aware of their grand with its newly invented action. But what was perhaps odd about their display is as follows: the piano appears to have been locked up for most of its time at the Exhibition, with the new action mechanism hidden away from anyone's prying eyes. We suspect this may have been due to the fact that Hopkinson's design was in fact closely modelled on the existing Erard system (with forked hammer shanks and an intermediate spring-loaded repetition lever, for example), and so perhaps the Leeds brothers were worried that they might be accused of infringement of another maker's patent, or at the very least be accused of plagiarism.

The jury at the Exhibition noted the unfortunate tendency of some of the makers to lock up their pianos so as to prevent the general public from seeing the innards. They noted:

- - - *We give this description from a pamphlet by the maker* [actually Henry Herz of Paris] *as the instrument itself being locked up, we could not obtain the opportunity of examining it. The same has been the case in other instances, and we cannot help remarking, that the practice of sending articles to the Exhibition, and refusing to exhibit them - - - - tends to defeat the main object of the Exhibition*.[6]

Newton's *London Journal* noted that:

Mr Hopkinson exhibits a grand, with a new action, called the 'patent repetition and tremolo check action', but as the mechanism is not shewn, we can merely remark that it is intended to give such an extreme degree of repeating power, that a kind of tremolo may be produced by slightly agitating the key when down. The dampers consist of wedges of soft cloth, on the German plan.[7]

If nothing else, these two sources of information give us some idea of the level of suspicion which rival makers held towards each other in the mid-nineteenth century. What certainly distinguishes the Hopkinson action design from any other, is a kind of 'flexible jack', which is in two parts and hinged centrally, a feature which is illustrated diagrammatically on the patent application[8] dated the 3rd June 1851. The design results in an extremely lively, sensitive and responsive touch, which is considerably superior to the Broadwood grand action of the same period, except for one feature: the Hopkinson action, because of its complications, is apt to be rather troublesome to keep in a good state of regulation when compared with the Broadwood equivalent.[9]

PATENT PIANOFORTES

MANUFACTURED BY

J. & J. HOPKINSON, 18, SOHO SQUARE.
LONDON.

These Superior Instruments received the Award of

The Great Exhibition Prize Medal
FOR PIANOFORTES, IN 1851,

And the Most Celebrated Pianists of the age have pronounced them "perfectly beautiful in tone and touch, and not surpassed by those of any other Maker;" as may be seen by Letters and Testimonials from

S. THALBERG.
JULES BENEDICT.
E. SZEKELY.
MADAME DULCKEN.

AND OTHER EMINENT MUSICIANS.

TO BE HAD OF ALL MUSIC SELLERS.

PRICES:

	GUINEAS.
Boudoir Piccolos, according to style and finish, from	25 to 60 each.
Cottages . . . . ,,	30 to 80 ,,
Patent Semi-Grand . . . . . . ,,	80 to 100 ,,
Patent Grands . . . . ,,	110 to 160 ,,

A mid-nineteenth century advertisement for Hopkinson pianos.
[Author's collection]

In recent years, the author has had the opportunity to take part in the restoration of a tall, wooden-framed Hopkinson 'cottage' upright from the 1860s. Both the design and construction of the instrument are very conventional, and show all the typical features found on uprights of the day: wooden framing, straight stringing, and 'sticker' action. What is striking about the instrument is its astonishingly strong and powerful tone, presumably the result of particularly high-tension stringing. A close scrutiny of the interior of the piano revealed the name GOWLAND stamped in capitals into the wooden facing at one end of the tuning plank. If Edward Gowland the factory foreman did not actually design the piano, then he will at least have checked over the instrument and 'passed out' the model on the completion of its manufacture, the stamped name being his seal of approval. Gowland is also remembered as being the inventor and patentee of the curved brass 'pressure bar', located between the tuning pins and top bridge, a notable contribution towards the evolution of the modern upright piano.[10]

The new Fitzroy Road factory, 1866

Number 44, Fitzroy Road, in the fashionable Primrose Hill district of Camden Town, is a rather surprising site for a piano works; and yet here, in 1866, Hopkinson decided to locate its new factory, in the middle of a row of elegant terrace houses. (Planning laws of today would have prevented this from happening!) Nevertheless, the façade of the factory blends extremely well with the houses to each side of it. The frontage has clearly been specially designed to be as imposing as impossible, its lavish features inspiring confidence from each and every customer visiting the premises. In fact, the Hopkinson façade, with its vaulted porch, is far more reminiscent of the entrance to some glamorous West End theatre or other, rather than being an entry into a hum-drum piano factory. We can be fairly certain that immediately inside the entrance, there would have been some kind of showroom area, with a variety of new pianos on display.

Behind the entry façade is a surprisingly commodious factory building, which extends to the rear of the entry on five levels and in length by a hundred yards. To the side of the factory is the former timber yard, containing a single-story building which is likely to have been the wood-machining shop. (Today, the whole premises are occupied by the Primrose Hill Community Association, and the narrow street adjoining is now, fittingly, called Hopkinson's Place.) In the spring of 1924, the firm of George Rogers and Sons, which had recently purchased Hopkinson, arrived to occupy the Fitzroy Road factory, and thereafter both Hopkinson and Rogers models began to be made under the same roof.

The upper photo shows the imposing façade of the Hopkinson piano factory, 44, Fitzroy Road, Primrose Hill, erected in 1866. The lower photo is a side view of the same building, showing workshops on five floors.

[Photos: Laura Little]

The later Hopkinsons

John Hopkinson, the senior partner, retired three years after the opening of the new factory, in 1869, and with his wife Charlotte, moved to a place remote from either London or Leeds: Criccieth in Carnarvonshire, north Wales. We have no idea why the couple chose this relatively remote place – they must have been seeking peace and quiet. John and his wife had not produced a family. He died on the 4th April 1886, an extremely wealthy man (he was worth over £20,000 as a result of his piano making endeavours, a sizeable fortune at that date). In his will made shortly before his death,[11] he made generous bequests to various nieces and nephews, leaving his valuable collection of violins and cellos to his nephew, James Hopkinson.

By this date, the family's now-famous piano making concern had been taken over by two more J. & J. Hopkinsons: two brothers, John the younger (c.1845-1919) and James the younger (c.1846-1924). They were the sons of the elder James, one of the two original business partners. What is apparent, however, is that as the nineteenth century progressed towards its conclusion, the second-generation proprietors distanced themselves more and more from the piano factory floor. James, for instance, had moved to St Leonard's-on-Sea on the Sussex coast by 1891. For a few years, he might have been able to commute daily into London; but he had married Isabella Garland, the daughter of a Scottish farmer, and in the year 1895 he used his accumulated wealth to purchase a country estate at Monaughty, Morayshire. Shortly afterwards, he was appointed a Justice of the Peace for the County of Moray.[12] Following his move to Scotland, he appears to have severed all his connections with the piano industry. Like his uncle John, he obviously preferred the peace and solitude of rural life to the dust and clatter of the piano factory floor.

The day-to-day running of the company was taken over by a certain William Wood, who became general manager. The elder Hopkinson brother, John, lived at Watford, and although nominally the head of the firm, his life's interest lay in the field of zoology, rather than in pianos. He was a Fellow of the *Zoological Society*, and had a string of distinguished qualifications after his name: FLS, FGS, FZS and FRMS. As *The Pianomaker* magazine commented, almost regretfully, in its printed obituary of him, in the edition of July 1919:

> Died on 6th instant, Mr John Hopkinson. He was the last of the Hopkinson family to take an active interest in the business. He was a director of the company up to 1913. Mr Hopkinson's inclinations lay more towards science than industrial life.[13]

The Hermitage brothers and Frank Challen, 1919-1924

Three months before the death of John Hopkinson, the piano manufacturing company was purchased by a business consortium comprised of George, Arthur and Donald Hermitage, and Frank Challen. The latter, a member of the well-known London piano manufacturing family, had been Hopkinson's technical director and factory manager since 1907. He had achieved a reputation as the designer of some of the finest upright pianos ever made in London. There is a full account of his life's activities, as well as a head-and-shoulders portrait of him, in *Five London Piano Makers*,[14] published by the author in association with Keyword Press in 2010. Challen's most outstanding design is his 'model 12', a large upright instrument, which won gold medals for J. & J. Hopkinson at the International Fairs at Brussels (1910) and Turin (1911). Frank Challen's illness and sudden death in hospital at the age of fifty-six in July 1919, three months after the Hopkinson takeover, was a sad and serious loss to the Hopkinson business.

The Hermitage brothers were involved with the commercial side of the Hopkinson business. They owned a highly successful family-run music shop, known as *Steven Hermitage & Sons*, at St Leonards-on-Sea, Sussex. There, they must have stocked not only Hopkinson and other makes of pianos, but also had a personal acquaintance with their near neighbour James Hopkinson before the latter left for Scotland. There is one small but interesting anecdote associated with this particular music shop: one day, the showroom received a surprise visit from the famous French composer, Claude Debussy, who was taking a holiday in the locality. He took a great liking to the Blüthner grand he saw on display, which he tried, and, on impulse, decided to purchase it from Hermitage & Sons, asking for it to be delivered by boat to his temporary home on the Channel Islands. Once there, the piano played an important role: it was used by Debussy as a work-tool in the composition of his well-known orchestral masterpiece, *La Mer*.

The Hermitage brothers came from a religious, modest and hard-working family; but although they appear to have been highly successful in the retailing side of the music industry, they might have been a little 'out of their depth' when it came to their purchase of Hopkinson. George Hermitage, the eldest, became general manager of the company; but the brothers had joined the piano manufacturing industry at a very difficult time for the Trade, immediately after the First World War, and they had lost, with Frank Challen's death, not only a technical foundation, but also an important link with the original company. The consortium had had to borrow some £17,000 from the bank in order to purchase Hopkinson, and although a profit had been made in 1919, the losses steadily began to accumulate:[15] in 1920, the firm lost £2,754; in 1921, £4,419; and in 1922 £1,309.

Following George Hermitage's death in October 1923, the firm ultimately went into receivership and voluntary liquidation at the beginning of the following year. It was stated that the cause of the collapse had been 'unsound trading'. In a desperate bid to maintain piano sales, J. & J. Hopkinson had deliberately lowered its prices, so that their pianos were actually being sold at less than manufacturing cost.[16] As a result of this practice of competitive 'under-cutting', the firm had quickly become extremely unpopular within the industry. A depressing list of eighty-three trade creditors, owed a total of £44,154 1s 8d, was printed in the February 1924 edition of *The Pianomaker* magazine.

(As far as the Hopkinson factory building in Fitzroy Road was concerned, this had not been conveyed to the manufacturing company, but remained in the ownership of a Trust set up by James Hopkinson the younger of Scotland for the benefit of his two unmarried daughters.[17] The premises were eventually sold by Hopkinson descendants in the 1950s.)

Early Rogers Days

George Rogers, the founder of the piano manufacturing business, was born in Chelsea, London, in or around the year 1822. He was a member of a 'clan' of piano makers, all called Rogers, who were active in the Euston and Camden Town districts of north London from the mid-nineteenth century. The London Post Office Directories reveal, for example, that a certain David Rogers was trading from Hampstead Road from 1847, and that a Henry Rogers was also trading from Hampstead Road from 1848, and a few years later from Warren Street. Then an individual named William Rogers had his piano workshop in Seymour Street, Euston Square, and a certain 'T. Rogers & Son' operated from Southampton Mews from circa 1850. We can be fairly certain that all these individuals were related in some way or other, but so far there has not been an opportunity to unravel the various family connections.[18]

George Rogers opened his business in 1843, shortly after completing an apprenticeship with Collard & Collard. For a number of years afterwards, the earliest Rogers pianos had the inscription *from Collard & Collard* applied to their nameboards, indicating that Rogers regarded his Collard training as a valued way of generating business goodwill. By the year 1860, trading as *George Rogers & Company*, he had become established at number 1, High

Street, Camden Town. This business address appears to have been a general music shop (selling sheet music and small goods as well as pianos), above which the family lived. The pianos themselves were constructed in a workshop a short walking distance away, in Gloucester Street, off Bayham Street.

When compared with Hopkinson, George Rogers' production was considerably smaller. During the early 1870s, for example, his piano output amounted to around five instruments per week, compared with Hopkinson's fourteen; by the mid 1880s, Rogers' weekly output had increased to something like nine, but the Hopkinson factory made sixteen. Shortly before the outbreak of the First World War, the Rogers firm's output was maintained at around ten each week; Hopkinson was making twenty. These figures are based upon a fifty-week working year, and use the various serial numbers found in Pierce Piano Atlas to estimate annual output.[19] But the Rogers company had been slowly expanding, and we can see this in the way it had opened a prestigious showroom and office at 60, Berners Street in the West End by 1892, as well as two branch retail shops by the same date, one in St John's Wood and another in Finchley Road. The old factory in Gloucester Street had been vacated, and a new factory specially built in Archer Street, Camden Town. (This same factory was to be occupied by Challen & Son from 1914.)[20]

George Rogers was eventually joined in business by his four sons. Of these, 'Tom' Rogers (born circa 1852) spent most of his working days managing the office and selling pianos at the Berners Street showroom, whilst his younger brother Charles (born c.1854) remained in charge of the Archer Street factory. The eldest son, George Thomas (born c. 1850) was also working for the business – as a piano tuner – in the early 1870s, but for some unknown reason he disappeared from the family concern shortly afterwards. The fourth son, Frederick (c.1856-1925), was given the responsibility of managing the retail branch in Finchley Road.

Samuel Wolfenden (1846-1929)
When commenting about the career and personality of Samuel Wolfenden (an author of two books about piano making and sometime manager of the Rogers factory)[21], the editor of *The Pianomaker* had this to say in the obituary included in his edition of April 1929:

- - - *An Englishman who was self-educated, but whose choice of words in both conversation and in writing exhibited the innate gentleness of his character. Mr Wolfenden had at some time been factory manager of the old George Rogers business, and a little later was appointed technical advisor to the Aeolian factory at Hayes, a post which he retained until his death virtually, as when he retired from active work in the factory the company made him a generous pension. Until last year the Music Trades School* [at the Northern Polytechnic] *had full advantage of the store of knowledge Mr Wolfenden was ever ready to impart, and the staff of the school and the students are the richer for his free liberality of thought. A groundwork has been left upon which future generations can build with security. 'Honest to God, honest to man'. That was the phrase used by the clergyman at his graveside.*[22]

Wolfenden came from a family long established in piano making. His grandfather, Phillip Skelton Wolfenden (born c.1782) was a native of Lisburn, Ireland, who had settled in London as a young man, where he found work in one of the factories as a piano action finisher. He had two sons: Samuel (born c. 1815), a piano tuner; and Robert (born c. 1832), a piano case maker. Samuel the tuner's wife Catherine was a schoolteacher, and this might help to explain how her son, Samuel junior, described in the above obituary as a 'self-educated' man, was nevertheless helped to acquire the necessary facilities to write two books about piano making. In the Census Return for the year 1901, Samuel junior, like his father, is described as a 'piano tuner', living at 7, Harrington Street, St Pancras, with his wife Emily. Apparently, he was not yet manager of the Rogers factory, but he is likely to have taken up this position within the next few years, as assistant and eventual successor to Charles Rogers of the 'old' company.

We have very little idea as to how Samuel Wolfenden acquired his enormous theoretical and practical knowledge about piano construction. Much of it must have been picked up from experience gained working on the factory floor. But he would have had access to one or

Samuel Wolfenden (1846-1929).
[Frontispiece from 'A Treatise on the Art of Pianoforte Construction' by Wolfenden, 1916]

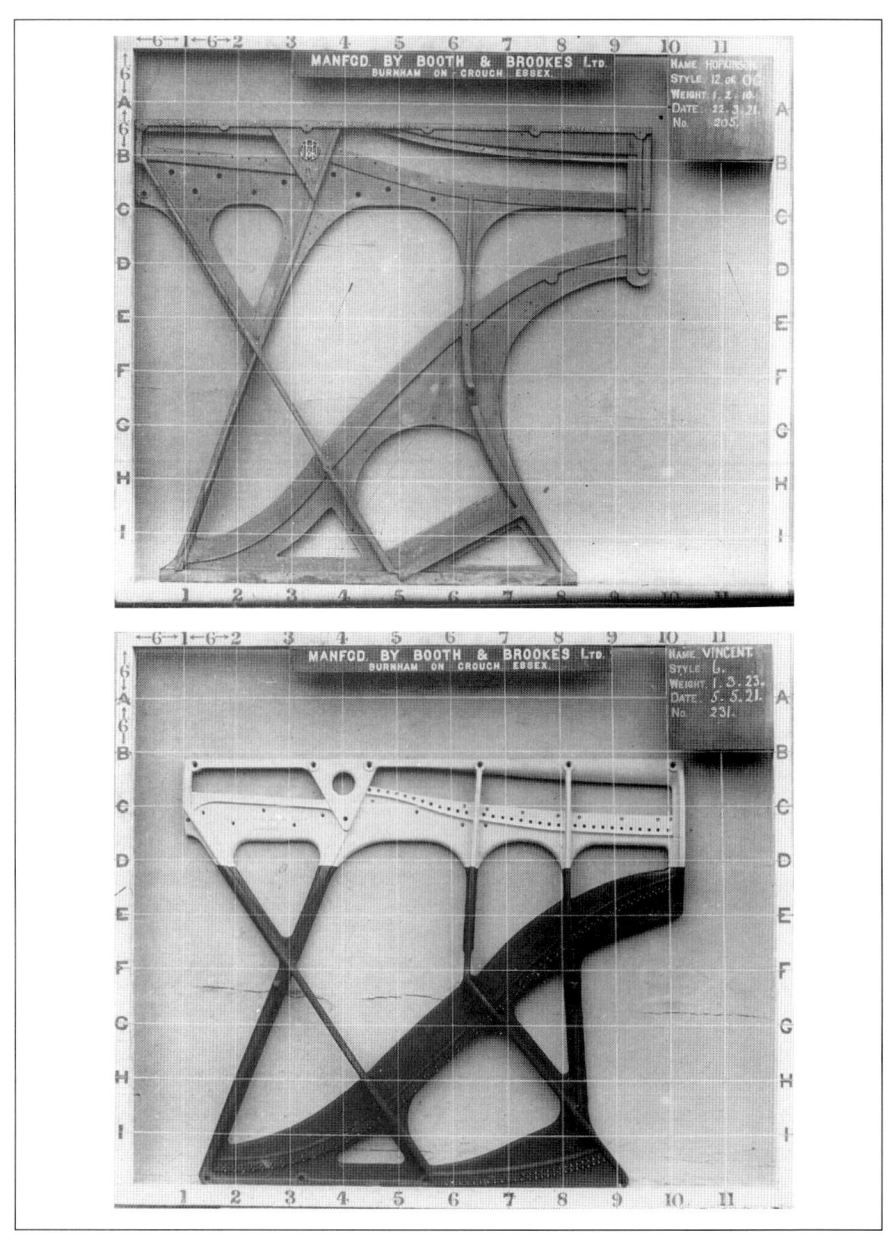

The cast-iron frames for two outstanding yet contrasting upright piano designs: the upper photo shows Frank Challen's Hopkinson model 12. The lower photo is of Samuel Wolfenden's Rogers model 6.

[Booth & Brookes ironfoundry archives, Essex County Record Office, Chelmsford]

two publications, such as the German Theodore Hansing's excellent theoretical treatise, *The Pianoforte* (1888), an English translation of which had been available from 1909. There was also a small handful of piano 'scale designers' working in the London piano factories during the closing decades of the nineteenth century. They must have been a very small 'elite', privy to the kind of specialist knowledge upon which every maker depended. We can name a few of them: Alfred Squire, Frank Challen, Horace Brinsmead, Theodore Wennberg, and Reinhold Glandt. Wolfenden may well have met all of them in the course of his work, and no doubt he would have been keen to discuss piano design with them in a casual way – and perhaps for hours on end.

The surviving examples of Rogers pianos incorporating Wolfenden's scale designs are quite distinctive internally: unlike almost every other London-made piano, his upright instruments have *two* iron bars in their treble sections, a feature certainly borrowed from Bechstein; and this would help to explain why the Rogers instrument became known as the 'English Bechstein' in the Trade, even though Wolfenden's scales are certainly not carbon copies of the Bechstein equivalent. The new models which Wolfenden was developing in the Archer Street factory soon brought fame to, and great respect for, the old Rogers firm. The accompanying two photographs are interesting, showing as they do the strikingly different features of an iron frame found in a Challen-designed Hopkinson upright, compared with the frame of a Rogers upright model of similar date, designed by Wolfenden.

By the early 1920s, Samuel Wolfenden, by now over seventy years of age and semi-retired, became a regular guest and advisor in the Piano Department of the Northern Polytechnic, Holloway Road. He must have been regarded by both students and staff as being some kind of piano-making 'guru', and is remembered as having a very diminutive stature (smaller than the majority of the students), but of strong personality, and anxious to be helpful. He would entertain the students with stories of his younger days in the industry, and with various problems which had faced manufacturers. When narrating an anecdote, his 'punch line', following a dramatic pause, was always his proud assertion: 'And then *I* was called in' (in other words, called in to solve matters). After a number of Wolfenden's visits, the young students on the Piano Course were by then at the ready for this customary punch line, and when it arrived, would cheekily join in – loudly in unison — much to the consternation of Wolfenden himself!

Dr Charles John Vincent (1852-1934)

Sometime around the year 1913, the firm of George Rogers & Sons was acquired by Dr Charles John Vincent. On first thoughts, we wonder if there had been some kind of close connection between members of the Rogers family and Vincent himself, which eventually led to the purchase; but in fact Vincent was investing and dabbling in other piano-making companies at the same time, including Challen and Eavestaff;[23] and so his particular interest in Rogers might have been seen by him only from the point of view of financial speculation.

What we do know is that Dr Charles Vincent was a very wealthy individual, with money available to speculate, although the actual source of his wealth is not presently known. He came from a musical and organ building background: his grandfather, Henry Sherborne, was a well-known organ builder from Bath, who for some reason had moved up to Sunderland on the north-east coast of England. Henry's Sherborne's son-in-law, Charles Vincent senior, opened a general music store at Bridge Street, Bishopwearmouth, county Durham. Charles Vincent junior, the eventual purchaser of Rogers, was brought up at Bishopwearmouth, then gained a doctorate in music from Oxford University, went on to became a well-known performing organist, and established a periodical known as *The Organist & Choirmaster*, which he ran between 1893 and 1919. By the year 1891, he had moved with his wife and children to Hampstead, London. Curiously, he became a piano manufacturer quite late in life: when he took the decision to purchase George Rogers & Sons, and establish *Vincent Manufacturing Ltd*, he was just over sixty years of age.

Once he had gained control of the Rogers company, Dr Vincent left the day-to-day running of the business in the hands of a certain Mr C. Sawyer, who became general manager. In contrast, Vincent appeared to lead the life of a playboy: he enjoyed travelling globally, visiting South Africa, Australia and New Zealand (as much for pleasure as for promoting sales of the Rogers piano), and he lived at Monte Carlo, Monaco, towards the end of his life. Nevertheless, it would appear to have been Vincent's capital investment in the Rogers business which had strengthened the firm, and which enabled a significant expansion. Between 1919 and 1921, there was a remarkable almost doubling of piano output, increasing from around ten to around twenty instruments per week.[24] It was against this strong financial background that the Vincent Manufacturing Company was able to take over the defunct J. & J. Hopkinson in March 1924, and move its production into the old but commodious Hopkinson factory in Fitzroy Road, Primrose Hill.

Uprights & Grands

When examining the history and development of the Hopkinson/Rogers enterprise during the 1920s and into the early 1930s, there is one disappointing feature we feel obliged to comment upon: the company appeared to make no effort whatsoever to produce a grand piano of more than five feet in length (152cm). Diminutive baby grands, usually of around 4' 6" (137cm) length, appeared to have been the mainstay. Vincent Manufacturing had clearly focused its grand output on the domestic market. The company appears to have had no ambition whatsoever to embark on the manufacture of larger models for professional concert use. Those Rogers and Hopkinson baby grands which have survived from the 1920s and '30s tend to have disappointing bass registers (in common with other grands of similar short length). The company was clearly responding to the demands of a certain section of the grand market – the safest, and probably the most profitable.

In contrast, Rogers/Hopkinson *upright* instruments from the same period are usually very good and highly thought of: they are well designed, robustly made, and as they are of a reasonable size (usually 122cm, or four feet in height, and above) their bass sections are usually musically quite acceptable. It was probably the range of upright models which maintained the Vincent firm's reputation for high quality, rather than its grands; and it is likely that the majority of the laudatory testimonials the firm received from various members of the music profession were for its upright models (see appendix 8.) During the 1920s and '30s, Rogers uprights were often the choice of the Royal Academy of Music, the Royal College of Music, the Guildhall School of Music, and Trinity College, London, for use in their numerous rehearsal rooms.[25]

We saw in an earlier chapter in this book dealing with the Chappell Piano Company that the Rogers/Hopkinson works manager during the early 1920s was Ernest Gowland, who then went on to become factory manager and director of Chappell from February 1926, taking with him his own designs which had hitherto been used to make both Rogers or Hopkinson instruments. Gowland was replaced in his role of technical director. The firm's manager, C. Sawyer, wrote to *The Pianomaker* in January 1926, as follows:

It will be of interest to your readers to know that Mr John Challen has joined this company in the capacity of technical director. Mr Challen is so well respected in the trade, both for his personality and his very considerable and practical knowledge of

Three views of a baby: the Rogers 'Junior' grand, length 137cm (4'6").
Upper: the 'standard' model in polished mahogany, with three squared, tapered legs.
Middle: the reeded six-leg version, in figured mahogany.
Lower: the cabriole-legged version, in white walnut.
[From George Rogers & Sons' promotional brochure, c.1938]

modern Pianoforte construction, that we are sure his many friends will wish him success in his new position.[26]

John Challen was the nephew of the highly acclaimed designer and factory manager, Frank Challen of Hopkinson, and his career has been dealt with in detail in the present author's *Five London Piano Makers* (2010). With all the Gowland-designed models apparently uplifted to Chappells, John Challen was obliged to create a range of new instruments from the drawing board. By the mid 1930s, four sizes of Rogers/Hopkinson upright were available, the smallest and least expensive being the model '56' (66 guineas), of 3' 11" (120cm) height. The most expensive, the model '6', was an imposing instrument costing 99 guineas, and was 4' 4½" (133cm) tall, an unusually large example from the period when almost every other London maker was attempting to make more compact varieties.[27] Clearly, the model '6' was a serious musical offering; it was certainly an expensive one, being almost twice the price of most other London uprights of the day.

A close examination of the Rogers/Hopkinson upright piano frames from the 1930s reveals that some of them have an uncanny resemblance to earlier frames employed in those *Steck* and *Weber* uprights made by the Orchestrelle Company Ltd of Hayes, Middlesex. We wonder if it had been possible for Challen to acquire these frame patterns after the Hayes company closed down in the early 1930s.[28]

A very welcome development at Fitzroy Road during the mid

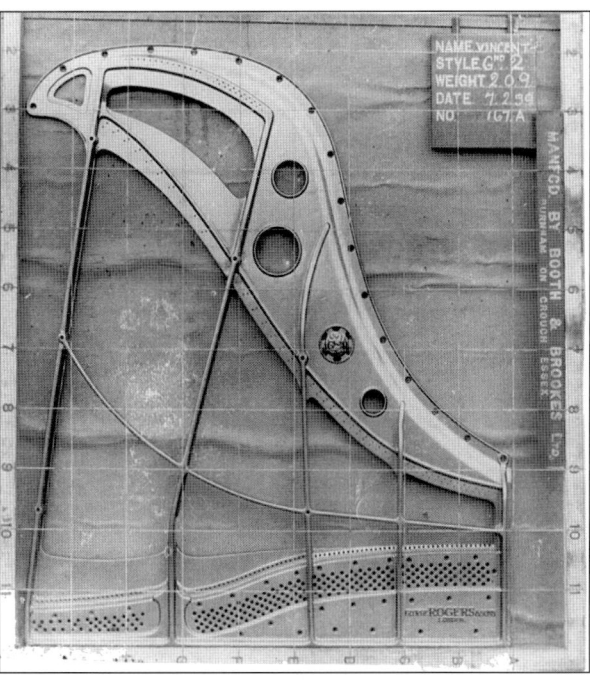

The cast-iron frame for the Rogers six-foot boudoir grand. February 1939.
[Booth & Brookes ironfoundry archives, Essex County Record Office, Chelmsford]

to late 1930s was the introduction of two significantly larger grand designs, perhaps for the first time in the history of the Rogers company: a *Boudoir* model of six-foot length (183cm), and an even larger *Drawing Room* model, of length 6' 8" (203cm). Tuners and technicians who have worked on these two instruments will confirm their excellent musical qualities. But these larger grands were undoubtedly made in very limited numbers, and because of their high price, will have had restricted sale.

Lanstein of Tottenham

Our knowledge about Rogers/Hopkinson activities immediately after World War II is unfortunately rather limited. We are not even certain whether any piano production, which had stopped for the duration of the War, recommenced at Fitzroy Road after 1945. All that we know at present is that the Vincent Manufacturing Company closed down in the early 1950s, vacated their address, and sold on the goodwill of the names Rogers and Hopkinson to the Lanstein company of Tottenham, north London.

The Lansteins operated a small piano manufacturing and repairing unit at 3-7, Springfield Road. The senior family member, Peter Paul Lanstein (1868-1946), had established workshops at Tottenham by the 1930s. It was his son and successor, Paul William Lanstein (1896-1964) who had purchased the Rogers/Hopkinson goodwill; but the latter's piano production was always to be on a surprisingly small scale. If the serial numbers are to be believed, Paul Lanstein was content to manufacture 1,451 pianos between 1950 and 1964, an average output of no more than one or two instruments per month over this long period. In fact, by the late 1950s, he had more-or-less given up piano making, and had turned his business into that of a successful general shopfitter's.[29] It is no wonder that by the early 1960s, the Rogers/Hopkinson business had become moribund.

Lowrey and Zender, 1963-1982

On the retirement of Paul Lanstein in 1963, things suddenly began to pick up: he had sold out to a business partnership comprising Herbert Lowrey and Ivan Zender. Capital was introduced. The new partnership moved its activities into the piano workshops recently occupied by G.A. Buckland and Company Ltd at Paxton Road, Tottenham, and probably utilising expertise gained from the surviving Buckland workforce, recommenced Rogers and Hopkinson manufacture there. New upright models were designed from the drawing board by Herbert Lowrey, a Berliner who had been trained at the family's Steinberg factory in the German capital, and who ran the manufacturing side of the new Tottenham enterprise. His business partner, Zender, was already the owner of a flourishing East London piano manufactory, Sydney Zender Ltd. Zender's role in the new firm was to be that of 'sleeping partner'.

The two new upright models which Lowrey designed were nothing like the Rogers/Hopkinsons of pre-War date: they were considerably smaller, they had simple, functional casework features, they were 'backless' designs (without any wooden back posts) and they were built down to an attractive price. This made the instruments very popular with the retailers. Many of the small Lowrey-designed instruments were offered in 'school' casework of oak, and proved to be very affordable for educational authorities when compared with the larger, better-made, but more expensive Danemann school models. But there was never any pretence at gaining the quality of the instruments made at Fitzroy Road twenty or more years earlier: the pianos were certainly built to a tight budget, which was also very much in line with the Zender company's policy of making small, low-priced instruments. Nevertheless, the new Lowrey-designed models were never as cheap as Zender's: in 1969, the standard seven-octave version of a Rogers/Hopkinson, costing £275, was some £40 more than the equivalent Zender. (This may be compared with a large Steinway upright from the same period, costing £684, or a new Blüthner upright, also of the same date, at £660. See appendix 11.)

The reminiscences of George Veness, a technician employed by Herbert Lowrey during the early 1970s, are included as appendix 9.

'Badge Engineering' under Bentley & Welmar
In 1982, the Lowrey/Zender partnership ceased trading, and both the Tottenham factory for the production of Lowrey models, as well as the East London Zender factory, closed down. This time, the goodwill attached to the names Rogers and Hopkinson was sold on to the Gloucestershire manufacturers, the Bentley Piano Company of Woodchester, near Stroud. Like the Zender, the Bentley piano was one of the cheapest available to the Trade, the small six-octave Bentley *Compact* upright being offered at the remarkably low price of only £199 retail in or around 1970. From 1982, the old-established Rogers and Hopkinson names were attached as options to the nameboards of the standard range of Bentley instruments, as requested by individual dealers. Sadly, there was never any attempt to produce a more expensive, up-market version bearing the newly acquired names, which might have revived the quality and standing which Rogers and Hopkinson perhaps still deserved within the industry. It was simply a matter of badge engineering, cashing in on the considerable amount of goodwill which the brand names Rogers and Hopkinson surprisingly retained at that date.

Following Bentley's liquidation and closure in 1993, the trade marks Rogers and Hopkinson passed to the London firm of manufacturers, Whelpdale, Maxwell and Codd Ltd, makers of the *Welmar* piano. Like Bentley, Whelpdales never made any attempt to develop any kind of 'quality' range of former Woodchester models: they simply continued where Bentley had left off, attaching the names Rogers or Hopkinson to the standard back and case designs of down-market Bentley origin. In the spring of 2003, the Welmar company went out of business, and the various trademarks it then owned were purchased by a firm of importers, *Intermusic Ltd*, of Poole, Dorset. Since that date, pianos bearing a variety of old English names, including Rogers and Hopkinson, have continued to be imported from China.

Afterthoughts

If we are to reflect on the changing fortunes of Rogers/Hopkinson since 1945, one thing is perfectly clear: the business, in whoever's ownership, was propelled forward by a substantial reservoir of long-established goodwill, which had been built up as a result of earlier decades of manufacturing instruments of high quality. This well-earned goodwill went a long way towards maintaining sales to the general public between the 1960s and 90s. (You can almost hear a loyal prospective customer entering a piano shop and, on seeing one of the new models, exclaiming: 'Ah, good old Rogers – still going strong!') The various enterprises which continued to manufacture Rogers and Hopkinson, whether Lanstein, Lowrey/Zender, Bentley or Welmar, made no attempt to enhance the reputation attached to these two marques. The instruments they manufactured functioned perfectly well, they were reasonably well finished, and they were certainly affordable. But they were built to meet the public's demand for smaller, simpler instruments available at a competitive price. It was 'market forces' which more than anything else determined the visual and tonal features of the post-War Rogers or Hopkinson piano.

We sometimes wonder whether things could have been very different. A particular manufacturer might have decided to revive the larger, high-quality Rogers/Hopkinson upright models offered at an earlier date. It would certainly have taken a very bold and fearless individual to have embarked upon such a radically different manufacturing policy. Inevitably, their instruments would have been highly priced, and because of their height and bulk, probably would have stuck out like a sore thumb on the piano showroom floor when compared with those very ordinary-looking little upright pianos which otherwise peppered the piano shops.

And yet, by the 1980s, the Japanese firms of Yamaha and Kawai were beginning to import substantially larger uprights which approached in dimension and tonal power those large London uprights made during the 1920s and 30s; and they were selling well. It just shows the level of 'paralysis' as regards innovation in the British piano industry when we realise that most of the surviving manufacturers were unable or unwilling to produce instruments in a size approaching those imported from Japan. The small, cramped, functional little British budget upright was all that their minds were willing or able to focus upon. If anyone had suggested to them a re-modelling of their product range along more traditional, up-market lines, they probably would have recoiled in horror, regarding such an option as 'suicidal'. Ironically, all these British makers have now long gone out of business; and the German manufacturers, who have survived, base their upright output on the type of larger, higher-quality instruments which for so long were rejected by the London manufacturers.

5
ALFRED KNIGHT

MANY years ago, when the author of this book was a young man, he attended a piano manufacturers' dinner in central London. It was held at the Strand Palace Hotel in the early 1970s. Seated at the top of the long dining table was the guest of honour, Mr Alfred Knight, then turned seventy years of age.

Before the dinner commenced, Mr Knight gave a short talk entitled something like *The Miracle of the Piano*. He moved to a raised stage area, on which was proudly displayed an example of one of his own make of upright instrument, and he proceeded to strum the keys for a few minutes – Knight on Knight. His playing was extraordinary: he produced a magical, sonorous tone quality, the likes of which the author had never quite heard before. The small upright was beautifully tuned and voiced. The other piano makers sitting at the long dining table were clearly captivated by the sound of the instrument, and listened in appreciative (and perhaps rather jealous) silence. After the performance was over, the spellbound author actually wanted to purchase a Knight piano! And it was also at this point that he suddenly understood how Alfred Knight had become such a successful piano manufacturer: he was a sales genius, using his extrovert charm and charismatic playing to sell his products.

Alfred Edward Knight came from humble origins: he was born at Camberwell, south London, on Boxing Day 1899. Both his father and grandfather were in the piano trade before him. His father, also named Alfred, was a 'regulating contractor' who hired out his services as a skilled piano action technician to the London piano factories.[1] One of Knight senior's regular workplaces was the huge factory of John Broadwood & Sons, which lay just over the River Thames in Horseferry Road, Westminster.

Alfred Knight junior, always known as 'Alfie', the eventual founder of the famous piano-manufacturing business, was a particularly 'bright lad'. At the age of thirteen, for example, he came top of his class of forty pupils at West Square Central Boys' School, Southwark.[2] Upon leaving school as a teenager, Alfie followed his family's occupation and became apprenticed to the long-established south London firm of makers, Henry Hicks and Son of Newington Butts. There, during his five-year apprenticeship, he would have learnt the necessary skills for piano tone production, such as stringing, action and keyboard installation, voicing of hammer felts, and then fine tuning.

Although notably small of stature, young Alfie was big-hearted and generous, with a warm, affable personality. But he was also remembered for his sudden bad temper, which usually only flared up later on in his life – if things started to go wrong in his own piano factory. He had other talents in addition to the bench-work skills he had acquired at Hicks & Son: as we have already noted, he was a remarkably accomplished pianist. But he was also gifted with a fine singing voice, a light tenor, not remotely operatic, but certainly attractive enough for variety cabaret entertainment. This particular talent – his singing voice – led Alfie Knight to contemplate a professional career as a music hall artist, and at one period in his youth he was actually spending a large proportion of his spare time energetically performing at a variety of evening venues in and around London.

Squire & Longson
Knight's fascination with piano making eventually gained the upper hand, however, and at the age of only twenty-four, in 1923, he was appointed a junior director of the south London firm *Cremona Ltd*, manufacturers at Medlar Street, Camberwell of the *Squire & Longson* and other brands of piano. (We have already encountered this firm in chapter 3 of this book.) Knight's particular role appeared to be that of assistant works manager, under Clarence Lyon and Charles Squire. He held the managerial position until 1931. It must have been a very stimulating job for him, as his employers at this period were open-mindedly experimenting with a number of new ideas in piano construction, and Knight was eager to participate in all the various developments.

We know that he played a role in the scale design of some of the Cremona product range, and that he also experimented with new types of cast-iron piano frame. For example, his design for the Cremona model C26 upright, dating from February 1927, shows how Knight was attempting to move away from the solid, heavy, 'plate' appearance of a traditional frame, in favour of a single casting which nevertheless had all the *appearance* of being constructed from an assembly of light, interlocking steel girders, welded together.[3] (The design and pattern of the C26 remained Knight's personal property, and so he was able to use the frame in some examples of his own make of piano after he went into business on his own account in the mid-1930s.)

During the late 1920s, then, the design of Cremona cast-iron frames was being deliberately modelled to give them a definite 'novelty' value for piano retailers and their customers – in an attempt to gain sales. We can see this, for example, in the design of the Squire & Longson model 4 baby grand, with its complicated clutter of interlocking iron ribs revealed when the lid of the piano is raised. The casual observer might have been led to believe that the instrument is actually stronger and more durable than it really is.

There is no doubt, however, that the kind of frame design being pioneered by Knight and others at Medlar Street results in a casting which is far more *rigid* than the traditional plate type. It was therefore much less dependent on the wooden back bracings for overall stability, and so the back bracings themselves could be slimmed down considerably in dimension. In an upright, they could begin to function largely as protection for the delicate soundboard immediately in front of them, rather than to function in any significant structural way. The overall depth of the piano case could then be reduced as well, making its outward appearance more compact and better proportioned. This particular concept of back construction – using rigid girder-type cast-iron frames – was utilised by Knight in his own models, dating from 1936 onwards.

Booker & Knight

In 1931, Knight left Cremona Ltd and began to take steps to establish his own piano-making concern. He found a business partner in the shape of a certain Mr Booker, the landlord and proprietor of *The Horns* public house at Kennington. Booker was of great help in financing the new business, but remained a 'sleeping partner', with no involvement at all in piano manufacture. He was an extremely wealthy individual, willing to invest and to speculate. *The Horns* was no ordinary public house, either: upstairs on four floors was a series of grand dining salons where lavish, high-quality catering, combined with live entertainment, was provided. Numbered among the regular guests was royalty, such as the future King Edward VIII, then Prince of Wales. It is highly likely that Knight had become acquainted with Booker and *The Horns* as a result of his own cabaret performances there. (Booker and Knight remained on good terms long after their business association had ended. On occasions, 'Old Man Booker' would be seen visiting the Knight factory, but it was only a social call, to meet his much younger friend and former partner, and to find out how the business was doing.)[4]

In the spring of 1932, the well-established and highly-respected piano manufacturer, Sir Herbert Marshall & Sons Ltd, makers of the *Marshall & Rose* piano, became financially insolvent and was forced out of business. The firm was particularly known for its tall, expensive upright models and for its equally expensive player pianos which carried the trade mark *Angelus*. The firm's original factory in Kentish Town, north London, closed down, and the goodwill attached to the name *Marshall & Rose* was purchased shortly afterwards from the receivers by a former director, Ernest Marshall, one of Sir Herbert's sons. He then relaunched the business as *The Marshall Piano Company Ltd*, trading from number 18, Orchard Street, off Oxford Street, London.

Ernest Marshall and his three new co-directors had no intention of opening another factory; they had no 'hands-on' experience of piano making, either. They were anxiously seeking a firm which would be willing to provide a new range of Marshall & Rose instruments, made under contract, which they could then sell in their Orchard Street showroom or elsewhere. In particular, the Marshall company was badly in need of a smaller upright model to replace those older designs, which although fine musical instruments, had become by the early 1930s hard to sell because of their high cost and unfashionably large size.

It was at this point that Alfred Knight stepped into the picture: the resources of his newly-established manufacturing business were offered and an agreement was signed up with Marshall; a company named *Marshall & Rose Piano Manufacturing*, proprietors Booker and Knight, commenced trading from workshops in Reading Lane, off Mare Street, Hackney; and within three months the Booker and Knight partnership had created a charming new Marshall & Rose upright, named the model BK1 (the abbreviation obviously standing for 'Booker's and Knight's first piano').

The way in which the BK1 model materialised is fascinating to observe: by some means, Knight was able to purchase the frame casting pattern and scale design which had been used by the firm of John Forrester from March 1929 to manufacture a highly successful small overstrung model. The design, known as the '910', appears to have been the property of a Birmingham iron foundry of the name Whitfield and Son; but as both Whitfield and Forrester had closed down their respective businesses by 1932 (Forrester went into compulsory liquidation in October 1931),[5] the design had become available for purchase. It was acquired and put to good use by Alfred Knight, becoming transformed into the Marshall & Rose model BK1.

Before going into regular production with the former Forrester model, Knight made a number of significant improvements to the original. What had been an 'open' tuning plank he replaced with the more dependable webbed and 'bushed' type; next, about 10cm of unnecessary wasted height at the top of the frame was removed from the design. Four large lugs were then attached as extensions to the lower edge of the casting. These latter features

The cast-iron frame for Booker & Knight's upright model BK1 (formerly Forrester), used in the manufacture of new Marshall & Rose pianos. July 1932.
[Booth & Brookes ironfoundry archives, Essex County Record Office, Chelmsford]

had the effect of raising the iron frame to its original height on the wooden back of the piano, whilst at the same time enabling the bass bridge and low end of the tenor bridge to be hiked up a further 10cm away from the acoustically dead bottom edge of the soundboard, so improving resonance potential. Finally, Knight added a straight, horizontal 'stiffening bar' to the cast hitchplate (which ran more or less parallel with the wooden mainbridge attached to the soundboard) in order to strengthen the casting. This notable addition was to become a standard feature of his later designs, both grand and upright. Within the iron frame, the string scaling remained in its original form. (For further clarification of these various technical modifications, a glance at the accompanying photograph might be useful.) The re-modelled Forrester piano went into production from July 1932.[6]

In spite of the fact that the BK1 model was likely to have been put together in something of a hurry (Marshall would have put Knight under pressure to have an instrument available as soon as possible), it is nevertheless a neat little design, relatively easy to construct, not *too* small, and very saleable in the 1930s when there was more and more demand for upright pianos of compact form. The resulting instrument is 112cm (3' 8") in height. For the next few years, it appears to have been the only Marshall & Rose upright instrument available. Many years later, in the mid 1980s, the same design, now known as either the *York* or the *London* model depending on case details, was re-launched as a 'budget' instrument by the Knight company. It was easier and cheaper to construct than the other models in the Knight range, and so it could be sold at a more competitive price.

Following on from the BK1 upright, Knight now turned his attention to grand manufacture for Marshall at Reading Lane. It appears that two 'relics' from the original Marshall company had survived: one, the jigs, patterns and templates to make a five-foot baby grand; and secondly, the similar wherewithal to produce a six-foot boudoir instrument. The design of the five-foot baby grand appears to have been re-modelled by the late 1920s, but the boudoir model needed up-dating.[7] Knight appears to have simplified the original frame design, and created a new bending buck for the making of the grand rim out of one continuous sweep of laminated wood (rather than a rim made with one or more jointed corners). The newly-remodelled six-foot boudoir grand featured prominently in Marshall's advertising during the early 1930s. By this date as well, Marshall & Rose had obtained a Royal Warrant. The Royal Household would not have been aware that their newly acquired Marshall & Rose was in fact manufactured quietly behind the scenes by Alfred Knight and his team of craftsmen at Hackney.

Smaller Marshall & Rose grands were asked for, and so during the early 1930s Knight created four new baby models, known respectively as the K2, K3, K4 and K5. The K2 (1933) is a very diminutive, conventional baby grand of length around 122cm (4 feet). The K3 (also from 1933) is a slightly longer model, of 137cm length (4' 6"); and the K5 (1934) is exactly the same as the K3, with the exception that the iron frame design is modified by removing one of the iron bars, so that it has the appearance of a 'semi barless' design. (We have no surviving information about the K4.) All these four designs of baby grand utilise a continuous 'capo d'astro' bar, which, forming an integral part of the cast-iron frame, bears downward pressure on all the strings, rather than employing individual brass agraffes for each note. Knight must have acquired his specialised expertise in baby grand design and construction as a result of his earlier experience at the Medlar Street factory of Cremona Ltd, which also made baby grands.

It is clear that Booker and Knight retained ownership of each of these new Marshall & Rose designs of baby model, including their rim bending bucks. This explains how Knight was occasionally able to go into grand production after he had established his own company, although the demand for his uprights was usually so great that he had no time available to develop grand manufacture. In fact, he made perhaps no more than fifteen individual baby grand models after 1936, which must have been something of a disappointment for him. There was often talk of commencing regular production of the type, but nothing came of the discussions.[8]

The Marshall company must have been very grateful for Alfred Knight's input of expertise. The new models of Knight design offered to the general public must have considerably helped to maintain the goodwill attached to the Marshall & Rose name. But Knight himself was becoming increasingly dissatisfied with arrangements, particularly those concerning the shared remuneration as a result of the Reading Lane enterprise. Knight felt that he was not receiving his fair share of financial rewards from his endeavours. Indeed, at one point it was suggested that a level of deception was going on, but no individuals were actually named. Nevertheless, Knight increasingly felt that it was time to move on, particularly as Booker, his financial backer, wished to resign from the partnership for personal reasons. We suspect that the whole enterprise was producing little financial satisfaction for either partner. Knight therefore decided to terminate his association with Marshall, and the Reading Lane workshop closed down.

Alfred Knight Ltd

Before disengaging himself from his Booker and Marshall associations, Knight was quietly designing and building a prototype upright piano at his home. This was to be the model K6, the first instrument made as a *Knight*. (The model numbering is clearly a logical follow-on from the one upright and four baby grands, whose design and construction he had previously been involved with.) We sometimes wonder how Knight was able to construct the K6 in such domestic surroundings. He would obviously have brought in components from elsewhere and assembled them somewhere within the walls of his house, perhaps in a spare bedroom. There was one particular operation, the attachment of soundboard ribs, which he was obliged to carry out in his domestic surroundings. A delightful tale is told by Knight's elder daughter, Sylvia: she remembers, as a small child, having to crawl under an elaborate 'forest' of 'go bars', which had been horizontally sprung and wedged between the two walls of the hallway leading to the family kitchen! The go-bars functioned as clamps, pressing into place during the gluing operation the necessary nine or ten ribs needing to be attached to the prototype soundboard, which was vertically positioned on one of the side walls. The hallway therefore doubled-up as a piano factory. The transformation of part of her home for this use must have tested the patience of Mrs Florence Knight, but thankfully it was only to be a temporary arrangement, until Knight had located a suitable factory.

Alfred Knight Ltd was registered as a limited company on the 9th July 1936, with capital of £2,000. The new firm soon found premises – at Granville Park works, Brettenham Road, in the centre of Edmonton, London N18 – where the business was to be based for the next twenty years. Knight's new financial backer, who replaced Booker, was the Barnes Piano Group, a large London-based retailer, with impressive showrooms in Oxford Street and with various branches all over the south of England. Barnes acquired a 50% financial holding in the new company. This arrangement soon proved to be highly unpopular with other piano manufacturers, who pointed out that Alfred Knight Ltd would have an unfair advantage over them as far as sales and distribution were concerned. (For example, Knight pianos could have been supplied to Barnes at a heavily discounted price in view of the fact that the latter owned half of the company.) The Barnes Group was certainly a large fish in a small sea. In response to the many complaints, the 50% Barnes financial share was passed over some years later to two brothers, Leonard and Ivor Clemence, who, as 'sleeping partners', were to retain a profitable interest in Alfred Knight Ltd for the next forty-five years. It should be pointed out that the Clemences did not play an active role in the business. Although they were

MORE LONDON PIANO MAKERS

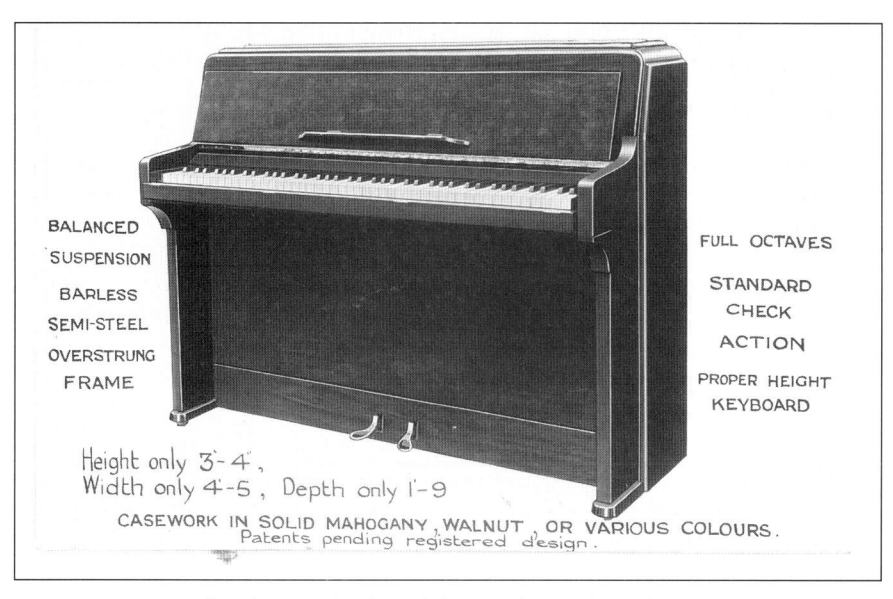

BALANCED SUSPENSION
BARLESS
SEMI-STEEL
OVERSTRUNG
FRAME

FULL OCTAVES
STANDARD CHECK ACTION
PROPER HEIGHT KEYBOARD

Height only 3'-4",
Width only 4'-5", Depth only 1'-9"
CASEWORK IN SOLID MAHOGANY, WALNUT, OR VARIOUS COLOURS.
Patents pending registered design.

An advertisement for the Knight model K6 upright, circa 1936.
[Sylvia & Michael York's Knight business archive]

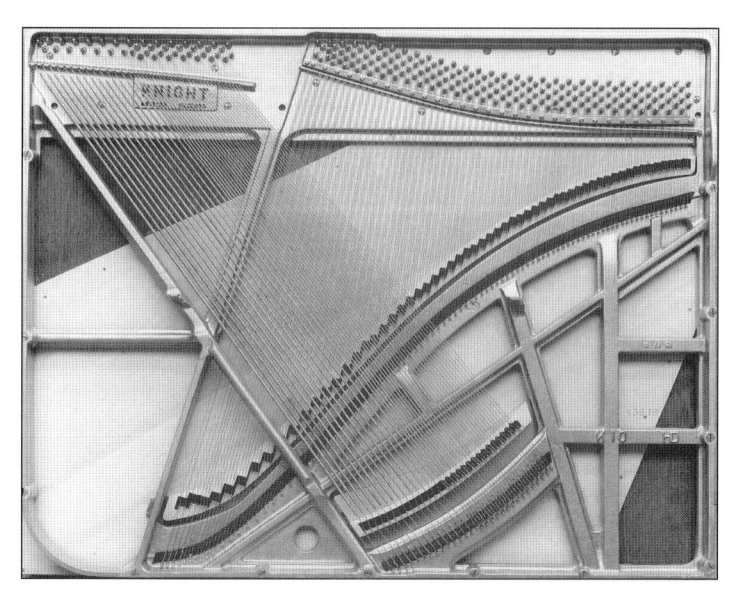

The strung back of a Knight model K10 upright, showing the cast-iron 'surround' frame. Note the unusual absence of the mid-treble iron bracing bar.
[Sylvia & Michael York's Knight business archive]

nominally directors of the company, they were neither piano builders, nor involved in any day-to-day administration of the firm.

The model K6

The first true *Knight* piano, the K6, is 107 cm high (3' 6") and has a seven-and-one-quarter octave compass. The first one, the prototype made in the Knight home, appears to have been given the serial number 1001; the second will have been 1002, and so on. During the first year of production alone, almost one hundred and fifty examples of the K6 left Granville Park works. During the following year, 1937-8, output increased to almost six hundred; then there was a further upsurge in numbers produced in the months leading up to the Second World War, when almost one thousand Knights appear to have been made annually.[9] It was a period of remarkable growth for the fledgling company. The little K6 had become very popular with the dealers: it was easy to sell on the showroom floor, partly because of its very reasonable price, initially retailing at 42 guineas (£44 and 4 shillings), partly as a result of its compact size, but also because each model possessed clear, bright, fresh, attractive tonal qualities.

But there was something else which contributed to these rapidly growing sales: unlike any other London piano manufacturer before him, Alfred Knight was keen to impart technical knowledge about his instruments to the dealers, and also to the general public. (Indeed, one of his sales brochures, dating from the early 1960s, entitled *The Heart of a Great Piano*, has more the character of a technical manual, than that of a glamorous sales brochure!) At first sight, this might seem to be a highly unorthodox method of trying to market a piano. But Knight realised that if the dealers had a fair smattering of technical information at their fingertips, it would help them to provide relevant back-up information to prospective customers. The tuners too would have appreciated written technical information which would have been of use and interest to them.

When Knight was asked to talk publicly about the merits of his pianos, he would frequently refer to his instruments as having 'the miracle of an audible seventh harmonic'. His audience would listen spellbound, even if they really didn't know what an audible seventh harmonic actually was! Another of Knight's selling ploys was to demonstrate the phenomenon of 'sympathetic pick up', which was a notable feature found in his instruments. He would hold down with one finger a low register key (for example a low 'D') but without playing it, on any particular instrument being demonstrated, and then immediately strike the same note two octaves higher with a staccato blow, played fortissimo. A few seconds would pass, and then, as if by magic, the low, un-struck and un-damped 'D' string would not only begin to 'sing' sympathetically, but its volume would steadily increase for a few seconds as it picked up the resonance imparted by the jolt emanating from the higher, staccato note. There were no upright models on the market in the 1930s which could achieve this impressive effect anything like as well as a Knight.

The question we must now ask is this: what were the special technical features of the Knight piano which made it such an attractive, saleable product? To begin with, its heavy 'all over' cast-iron frame was perhaps its most distinctive internal feature (see the photograph on page 88). It was certainly the heaviest piano frame for small uprights in general circulation from the mid 1930s, and the notable depth of its various cast members made it extremely rigid. (We recall how Knight had been experimenting with such frames at Cremona Ltd a number of years earlier.) The cast frame is firmly attached to the soundboard, and surrounds the board on all its edges, which means that there is an immediate 'reflection' or 'bounce back' of the board's resonance returned back into the soundboard. This feature largely contributes to the brightness and brilliance of the K6's tone.

But Knight was not the only maker in the 1930s making pianos with a considerable quantity of iron in their back construction: from 1932, the firm of Monington & Weston began manufacturing *very* heavy uprights and baby grands in which the usual wooden back bracings are replaced with a slim, secondary cast-iron frame, bolted to a front frame which supports the stringing load.[10] These particular pianos have the same sort of fresh, brilliant tonal quality as the K6.

The Knight cast-iron frame also has one special feature, which no other upright or grand had at this date: it is without the customary mid-treble bracing bar or girder. This object, deemed necessary by all other manufacturers, crosses through the long wooden, pinned mainbridge via a trough. As a result, there is often an unfortunate 'bump' in the piano tone where this trough occurs, and sometimes the strings serving the notes on each side of it can lack sustain and power – the result of the trough's interference with the vital transmission of sound along the length of the bridge.

The absence of the cast bar in the mid-treble of the Knight piano certainly helps the establishment of a smooth and even tone quality throughout the various registers, and aids the development of the kind of special 'pick-up' sympathetic resonance we noted in an earlier paragraph. Knight was not

A young apprentice preparing a keyboard for installation into a Knight piano. Granville Park works, Brettenham Road, Edmonton, London N18. Late 1930s.

[Sylvia & Michael York's Knight business archive]

the first to make pianos incorporating such a 'barless' feature: for about fifteen years from around 1906, the firm of John Broadwood & Sons manufactured 'barless' uprights, utilising a malleable steel frame; but these had been extremely expensive items to produce, which led to their discontinuation soon after World War I due to the very high cost of steel at that date.[11] And so, although not actually the originator of the barless conception, Knight was nevertheless successfully incorporating it into very reasonably priced pianos from 1936; and in all his later newly-designed models, whatever size of strung back, the mid-treble bar is conspicuously absent from the iron frame.

There is another technical feature which appears to have been an exclusive Knight detail, or at least one not generally adopted by London or other European manufacturers: this was the *'equal* tension scale'. In a *conventional* scale design of string lengths and thicknesses, there is always a noticeable rise in string tension as a change to a thicker wire gauge occurs: the first of the lower strings employing the thicker gauge of wire can sound a little louder than the strings serving the last note of the thinner gauge, one semitone above. This is usually not a serious problem, but, without going into too much technical detail, it can sometimes lead to inequality of tone at the point of gauge change over. The Knight stringing scale is designed to have exactly the same amount of string tension in each note, whatever the gauge of wire employed, and in whichever part of the keyboard compass a gauge change occurs. In theory, this 'equal tension' feature can enhance tuning stability and ensures a decided evenness of tone quality throughout the octaves.

Michael Cockram, writing in *Music Business* magazine of September 1990, had this significant comment to say about the Knight:

> *The Knight piano has occupied a unique niche in the British piano industry. It has always remained slightly apart from the mainstream of our piano production; there has ever been something indefinitely different about the Knight product. Other brands can boast of high standards, of reliability, of intrinsic tonal quality, but somehow a Knight has remained a piano apart. This was due in large part to the idiosyncratic genius of the founder of the firm - - - -* [12]

The NAAFI piano
At the beginning of World War II, Alfred Knight Ltd had a high level of stock and components, and this certainly helped the company to continue a normal level of manufacturing throughout most of the War period, whereas

all the other piano factories, apart from the Welmar works at Clapham, were obliged to close. Continuity of manufacture at Granville Park works at this difficult time was aided by the fact that Knight was commissioned to supply numerous pianos to the NAAFI (Navy, Army and Airforce Institute) and also to the British and American Red Cross. It has often been said in the Trade that Knight pianos, in view of their heavy construction, are 'built like tanks'; and the special models supplied to the NAAFI and the Red Cross, on behalf of the War Effort, were certainly no exception: they were made to be as robust as possible, to withstand the heavy wear and tear expected of them as they were strummed and thumped in the various military clubs and canteens up and down the country. The basis for this special model was a new back design, the K10, which was almost identical to the K6 except for the fact that it was taller by 8cm (3"), resulting in an enhanced quality of bass tone. After the War, this same K10 back was to be the foundation of a special 'school' model which began to be manufactured in considerable numbers.

The outer casework of the NAAFI model, constructed mainly from solid, heavy oak, has a number of almost comical features. The top of the instrument is deliberately constructed in the form of an angled 'shed', to prevent beer glasses from being placed upon it. It is also screwed into place to prevent it from being casually raised. The two pedals are backed by a heavy brass plate, to prevent the bottom door from being smashed to pieces by inebriated feet. Ashtrays are attached to the exterior at critical points; and the keys are covered in a flame-resistant material to reduce the risk of cigarette burns igniting the whole keyboard.

International Expansion

Towards the end of the War, as Knight's stocks ran low and more members of the firm's workforce were called up for active service, the output of instruments was reduced to a trickle: no more than a couple were made each week; but by the year 1950, annual production had risen to around eight hundred. This expansion had been largely the result of the deliberate development by the firm of a vigorous export trade. In fact, at this period, it was only by purposefully exporting that the majority of British piano manufacturers could survive: the home market in the UK had more or less dried up. Over 90% of Knight's output went overseas at this date.

Alfred Knight Ltd's curious policy towards exports was unique: no other British piano manufacturer appears to have thought of it; and it was certainly a very clever idea: the firm would now supply 'flat pack' kits of materials, piano parts and sundry components to overseas factories, which would then assemble and finish them, for sale in their own, or neighbouring, countries. A 'flat pack' was likely to contain a wooden back to which the iron frame was attached, a complete set of loose case parts in finished dimension, a set of wound bass strings, an action, a keyboard, and a set of felt-covered hammers; and then the necessary sundry smaller components, such as tuning pins, hinges and castors, would be included in the 'kit'. The assembly of all these items into a complete piano in an overseas 'satellite' factory would involve stringing up, assembling together the various case parts, installing the action mechanism and keyboard, polishing the exterior casework, and finally regulating, tuning, and voicing. Any piano made under this arrangement would *not* bear the 'Knight' name, but would display externally the name of the satellite assembling firm. The interior iron frame, however, would retain the Knight logo, cast into it.

**In the land of the giants: Alfred Knight (second from left) with the team of Norwegian craftsmen from the Grøndahl company.
In front, a Grøndahl/Knight piano is in course of construction. Oslo, circa 1950.**
[Sylvia & Michael York's Knight business archive]

The first firm to become such a 'satellite' was a well-established pianomaking business named Grøndahl, of Oslo in Norway, run by Anders Backer. On one occasion, during a visit to the Norwegian factory, Alfred Knight became irritated and angered by the fact that the Grøndahl/Knight instruments were looking and sounding better than his own instruments made in London! The second to become a similar satellite was the South African firm of C. Bothner & Sons Ltd, whose factory, situated in Johannesburg, was being directed by 'Bobby' Bothner. Knight had this to say about the factory's location:

> *The attraction of South Africa is the climate, so that the timber used can be perfectly seasoned. A humid climate is hopeless, so is a completely dry one. Johannesburg is perfect – a low moisture content, but just enough to keep the wood in the right condition.*[13]

The reason why the establishment of these export satellite factories was such a clever idea is a follows: it meant that the Knight company was able to purchase much larger quantities of stock (far more than its own London factory could ever process) therefore resulting in a welcome reduction in unit cost of each bought-in item. On one occasion, for example, the Burnham-on-Crouch, Essex, firm of iron founders, Booth & Brookes Ltd, opened its morning mail to discover an order from Alfred Knight Ltd for exactly one thousand piano frames! The order must have been a great delight to receive. Apparently, the Essex foundry had never received such an enormous order before; but it was obviously obliged to give a generous discount on the charge made for each frame eventually supplied.[14]

But Alfred Knight, unlike almost all other London manufacturers, also had his eye on the vast American piano market. There was another reason for his interest in the USA: his younger daughter Brenda (Mrs Rauner) had emigrated there with her American-born husband, and so Knight was able to combine a business trip with a pleasurable family meet-up. His first attempt at entering the American market, at the Trade Fair held at the New York Hotel, New York, in July 1952, was beset by setbacks, which were later recorded in an article in *The Daily Mail* of the 11th February 1955:

> *He took his piano to a convention – only to find that he had been left out of the catalogue and had been given a stand on the ninth floor when the show ended on the eighth. But he was determined to succeed. So he offered $1000 dollars and a new piano to anyone who could make a better one. He did not have to pay out. And now his piano is going into hundreds of American homes each year.*

***Knight reflects on his new model K15 spinet upright, initially manufactured for the
American market. Photo circa 1955.***
[Sylvia & Michael York's Knight business archive]

Specifically for the American market, Alfred Knight introduced a new model of piano: the K15, the shortest piano the firm had so far made, standing at only 96cm (38 inches) in height. This particular model was internally fitted with a special 'drop' action, and externally clad in the 'spinet' style casework which was very popular in the States during the 1950s. (An even shorter spinet model, having only a five-and-a-half octave compass, was introduced in July 1957, but as there was very little saving in construction costs in spite of the compromised compass, it was decided to discontinue the design shortly afterwards.)

The move to Loughton

Just as the idea of 'satellite' factories was part of a carefully thought-out long-term plan on the part of the Knight company, so was the planning and development of a new factory some way to the north of London. In June 1949, Alfred Knight Ltd took out an eighty-year lease on a 1.35 acre greenfield site at Langston Road, Debden Estate, Loughton, Essex. The plan was to eventually move the whole of the production from Edmonton to the Loughton site, but this was actually done in a very piecemeal way, spread over the next ten years, as funds for new building work became available. Extensions were gradually added on to the nucleus unit first erected at Loughton, which initially functioned as a 'finishing shop': partially-completed instruments would arrive here from the Granville Park works to be polished, have their actions and keys installed, and then be tuned and regulated prior to despatch. The original Edmonton factory continued to be primarily engaged in the 'donkey work' of wood machining, veneering, soundboard making, and case-part making. Logically, the necessary components for the numerous exported 'flat packs' would also be made and despatched directly from here.

The Debden Estate factory reached its final extent in 1959: the last stage of the development, costing some £20,000, enabled an overall increase in production space of about one quarter. The Granville Park works closed down, and by 1961 Langston Road, Loughton, had become the new headquarters of the company. The few years before the final move also coincided with the greatest-ever level of output of Knight pianos: during the period 1956-59, the firm was able to turn out, for the first time, more than two thousand instruments each year. It never attained this level of output again, apart from during the year 1974. An average annual production figure between the years 1961 to 1979 of 1,780 pianos, was nevertheless a remarkably steady and consistent level of output over this eighteen-year period.[15] Throughout the 1960s, approximately ninety people were employed

Downtown Toronto, Canada: an impressive display of Knight pianos for sale, circa 1960.
[Sylvia & Michael York's Knight business archive]

At Frankfurt Trade Fair: a jovial Alfred Knight is seated at the piano. His son-in-law, John York, stands on the left – circa 1960.
[Sylvia & Michael York's Knight business archive]

at the factory, and 80% of the firm's output continued to be exported.[16] By the year 1967, the company's overseas sales had amounted in annual value to £750,000.[17]

Recognition

For his remarkable services to exports, and also for 'promoting music in foreign countries', Alfred Knight was awarded an OBE in the New Year's honours list of 1966. Knight himself described his chief recreation, certainly a curiously rare one, as 'lecturing on piano manufacture throughout the world'(!)[18] As the 1960s progressed, the general public was becoming increasingly aware of the existence of the Knight piano. This had been greatly helped by the highly popular Beatles' film *A Hard Day's Night*, (1964), in which Paul McCartney was seen to be playing a model K10, its maker's name, proudly displayed above the keyboard, perfectly visible for all filmgoers to see. There was also an impressive, growing list of distinguished celebrities who owned Knights: the cellist Rostropovitch, the violinist Yehudi Menuhin, the jazz pianist George Shearing, and the singers Julie Andrews and Adam Faith. Spike Milligan chose one as well; and the actor Peter Sellers (clearly a fan) went overboard and decided to purchase three examples of the type.

It is very easy to forget that Alfred Knight's remarkable success had been greatly aided by the very high level of skill of his workforce. He had been very lucky in this respect. His workforce appreciated 'Alfie's' affable and humorous personality, the encouragement he undoubtedly gave them, and his insistence on the highest possible standards of workmanship. They returned this with great loyalty. We can mention, for example and in particular, Alfred's cousin, Jack Knight, who was highly recognised for his skills as a soundboard and back maker at the Granville Park workshops and who, quietly working behind the scenes, helped to maintain high standards. Alfred's other cousin, Harry Knight, was manager at the same place and contributed greatly to a satisfactory working environment. A select list of a few of those key personnel employed at the two Knight factories is shown in appendix 10.

As Alfred Knight's health deteriorated during the early 1970s (he was suffering from cancer) and he was no longer able to be involved in the day-to-day running of the firm as he would have wished, his elder daughter Sylvia and her husband John York took on the mantle and responsibility for the continued running of the business. Ultimately, Knight's illness took its toll and he sadly died on the 3rd September 1974, at the age of seventy-four. Writing in the *Journal of the American Piano Tuners' Guild*, two months later, Bernard Comsky commented:

Alfred's wonderful charm and wit endeared him to everyone who had the good fortune to know him. One could not walk with him at a convention more than a few feet at a time without having to stop and wait while people greeted him and shook his hand. He had that rare quality of creating a scintillating and exciting atmosphere wherever he went and could hold any audience with a particular cabaret act. With a technical audience his favourite trick was to sustain the fundamental and let the audience hear the harmonic series as he quipped 'You can't do this on an electronic organ!' Pianos were his life.[19]

Michael Cockram, again writing in *Music Business* of September 1990, had this to say:

Following his [Knight's] untimely death, his daughter Sylvia took over the reins, ably assisted by John York (her husband) and later by their son Michael. She strove, with great success, to maintain her father's high standards. It has to be said that without Sylvia York's total dedication and enthusiasm the firm could not have continued. Her warm charisma and sheer hard graft, with loyal support from her family, have kept the Knight name at the forefront of British pianos.

But Sylvia and John York, along with every other British piano manufacturer, were beginning to face increasingly difficult times for the Trade from the late 1970s: there was a large increase in competition from much cheaper pianos made in the Far East, leading to a fall in orders; and the demand for school pianos, which had been such a mainstay of Knight production and involved thousands of examples of the model K10 strung back, more or less collapsed as a result of a disastrous shrinkage of the schools market, the result of changes in national education policy.[20] From 1981, a Loughton output of only around five hundred pianos per annum was usually achieved, but without any reduction in overheads. Facing an increasingly difficult economic situation, the Knight directors had no option but to to close their factory – on the 31st October 1990.

Life after Loughton
Following the Loughton closure, the goodwill of the Knight name, along with a number of the designs of Knight piano, were conveyed to the Bentley Piano Company of Woodchester, near Stroud, Gloucester, where production of the K10 continued – but only for three years, as Bentleys themselves closed down in 1993. The Knight goodwill and designs were then in turn sold on to the London firm of Whelpdale, Maxwell and Codd Ltd, makers of the *Welmar* piano. At their works in Clapham, south London, Whelpdale continued to make a limited number of Knight instruments, usually never more than a couple of examples each week although the original unique strung back design of the K10 was retained and utilised. The Welmar company in turn closed down in 2003, and thereafter pianos bearing the trademark 'Knight' have continued to be imported from China by *Intermusic Ltd* of Poole, Dorset. Although bearing the Knight name, these imported instruments have no resemblance to the original designs formerly made in the London, Loughton or Woodchester factories.

Postscript
Up to the 31st October 1990, the history and development of Alfred Knight's business can certainly be regarded as an outstanding success in the world of piano making. If we are to analyse the underlying reasons for such a remarkable period of achievement, spanning over fifty years, we can compress our thoughts into the briefest of summaries: Alfred Knight offered a unique kind of inspired leadership in the British piano industry, coupled with technically sound piano design and astute marketing. These virtues were then successfully welded to the high level of craftsmanship coming from his loyal and dedicated workforce. The result was a remarkable business evolution between 1936 and 1990.

Alfred Knight OBE (1899-1974)

NOTES

1. THE CHAPPELL PIANO COMPANY

1. The author wishes to express his warmest thanks to Marie Kent for the painstaking research work she has undertaken on the author's behalf. She has spent a considerable number of hours sifting through back copies of *The Pianomaker* magazine, 1914-1931, held at the Periodicals Library, Colindale Avenue, London NW9 5HE.

2. Quoted in: *The Chappell Story* by Carlene Mair. Published by Chappell & Co Ltd, 1961.

3. The precise dimensions of the Phoenix Street piano factory are given in a report (following the factory fire) in the *Morning Chronicle* of the 6th November 1860.

4. Detail from a report on the factory fire, also printed in the *Morning Chronicle*, 6th November 1860.

5. An estimate of the Chappell output from 1840 to 1900 is based on serial numbers shown in *Pierce Piano Atlas*, published by Larry E. Ashley, P.O. Box 20520, Albuquerque, New Mexico 87154 - 0520, USA.

6. Source: see 3 & 4, above.

7. See 5, above.

8. London Census Return, 1881.

9. Probate documentation of Thomas Shepheard Mugridge of Bishopsteignton, Devon, gentleman, formerly of Belmont Street, Chalk Farm Road, Middlesex. Will made 26th August 1895, proved 27th January 1896.

10. From *Memories of Sixty Years in the Timber and Pianoforte Trades* by Louis Bamberger, published by Sampson, Low, Marston and Co Ltd, undated, c.1930. His family company, Bamberger & Son Ltd, supplied the London piano trade with specialist timber for soundboard manufacture. At one period, c.1900, Louis Bamberger was also chairman of piano makers J. and J. Hopkinson Ltd.

11. London Census Return, 1881.

12. Glandt family information kindly provided by David Pescod, R.F. Glandt's great-grandson.

13. The Application for British Citizenship from Reinhold Friederich Glandt is dated the 12th March 1900. Naturalisation was granted on the 17th July of the same year. (Source: David Pescod family archive – see note 12.)

14. Interesting information contained in a letter to the author from Ferguson Hoey of Norwich, dated 12th March 2014.

15. From a report describing the official opening of the Chappell factory extension on the 1st December 1920, contained in the edition of *The Pianomaker* magazine of the 15th December 1920.

16. Chappell serial numbers from *Pierce Piano Atlas* (see also note 5).

17. An obituary for Reginald Neale (with a photographic portrait) was printed in the edition of *The Pianomaker* magazine, November 1926.

18. Further details of Reginald Neale's life, career, and importance to Chappell, were received by the author in conversation with the late Charles Gilbey (1907-1980), a former Allison employee.

19. For further information about the Gowland family of piano makers, see also the chapter in this book dealing with the Rogers and Hopkinson firms.

20. For details about the work of John Challen in the industry, see: Alastair Laurence, *Five London Piano Makers* (Keyword Press: 2010, reprinted 2012), pp. 35-36.

21. For the prices of these various models, see the list which appears in appendix 2.

22. Chappell's purchase of the goodwill of Allison Pianos took place in April 1929, two months before the American take-over, but it is highly likely that the future American parent company was negotiating behind the scenes on Chappell's behalf. The goodwill of Collard & Collard Ltd was acquired on the 31st December of the same year. As a result of the Collard purchase, Chappell also acquired the brand name *Kirkman*. The Belmont Street factory then continued to manufacture pianos bearing the names *Allison, Collard & Collard* and *Kirkman*, as well as *Chappell*, through to the date of the closure of the factory in 1970; but these were all Chappell designs/models

with the various optional names 'badged' on them. In other words, there was absolutely no difference in internal technical specification between the Chappell models and models with the three other brand names attached. Only small stylistic details of casework, or the particular shade of bronze for the cast-iron frames, distinguished one brand from the other. For extensive details about the history of the Collard company, the reader is referred to: *Five London Piano Makers*, by Alastair Laurence (2010), pages 51-72.

23. See note 21.

24. Information received by the author in a letter from the late Percy Cossins of 28, Church Street, Messingham, Scunthorpe, dated the 18th May 1987.

25. The story of the 'Chappell Blüthner' was told in conversation to the author by the late Sydney Paradine, a piano tuner who had worked for over forty years in the Belmont Street factory.

26. Chappell serial numbers, again from *Pierce Piano Atlas* (see note 5).

27. Ralph Ralphs, Chappell's senior grand finisher, was born in Kensington, London, in 1881 and died on the 15th September 1975, aged 94. His name occurs in the London Census Return of 1901, when he is already shown as being a nineteen-year-old piano maker. In 1963, aged eighty-two, he was continuing to work part-time at the Chappell factory – he was the only grand finisher working for the company at that date. Without his part-time presence, there would have been no Chappell grand production at all.

28. In 2010, the old Victorian factory of the Chappell Piano Company was threatened with demolition. Its owners wished to apply for planning permission to completely redevelop the site. A campaign to oppose the demolition proposals was launched by local residents, led by the Camden councillor, Matt Sanders. A huge petition in opposition was raised, containing hundreds of signatures. Following a public planning enquiry, the enquiry's inspector threw out the demolition plans on the 3rd February 2011. The developers then considered an appeal; but thankfully, on the 19th April 2011, and in the face of intense pressure, they ultimately withdrew their application. The latest plans (2014) entail the remodelling of the old factory premises to function as attractive offices and flats.

2. EAVESTAFF, BRASTED BROTHERS AND THE *MINIPIANO*

1. From *Memories of Sixty Years in the Timber and Pianoforte Trades*, by Louis Bamberger, published by Sampson, Low, Marston and Co Ltd, undated c.1930.

2. Probate records for William Glen Eavestaff of 2, The Avenue, Brondesbury, Middlesex, who died on the 10th February 1912. Probate to Mary Eavestaff, widow, Amy Constance Eavestaff, spinster, and Stanley Lionel Eavestaff, artist. Value of estate: £6,101 14s 11d.

3. A photograph of Frank Eavestaff appears in the edition of *The Pianomaker* magazine of March 1923. He is shown attending the British Industries Fair, at which W. G. Eavestaff & Sons had a stand.

4. Brasted family information has been kindly provided by Robert Brasted, great-grandson of Henry G. Brasted, who founded the piano-making company.

5. An advert in *The Pianomaker* of April 1924 includes a small sketched view of the new factory. The wording of the advertisement states: *The capacity of the Brasted works is enormous. In organisation and efficiency it is without parallel. Yet even this is hardly sufficient to meet a demand which never stops growing week by week, month by month. Coping with the persistently increasing demand is one of the penalties of success. But the moral is this: let us know your requirements well in advance. This greatly helps us, saves rushing orders through, and gives satisfaction all round.*

6. A letter from Douglas Brasted to the author of this book, dated the 14th February 1962, includes the closing sentence: *If you are in London, please do not hesitate to ring to make an appointment to look round our works, said to be the largest in Europe.*

7. The serial numbers and manufacturing dates are contained in *Pierce Piano Atlas*.

8. A photographic image of the Erbe-Maas cast-iron piano frame appears in the records of Booth & Brookes, ironfounders, of Burnham-on-Crouch, Essex. At the top right-hand corner of the photo, the name 'HICKS' appears, hand written in capitals on a chalk board, so identifying the name of the piano-making firm which had ordered the type of casting illustrated. (*Essex County Record Office, Chelmsford. CM2 6YT.*)

9. These interesting testimonials appear in an illustrated brochure promoting the Eavestaff minipiano, date c.1936. (*Author's collection.*)

10. The production numbers quoted here, which are also serial numbers, are recorded in the purchase book of *Wigmore Hall Piano Galleries*. This piano retailer ordered a total of nine mini models between January 1935 and April 1939. (*Author's collection.*)

11. A list of events in the career of John T. Davis is recorded in a hand-written notebook compiled by Davis after 1970. The details are:

>   1914-1916: Imperial Piano & Organ Co, London Fields.
>   1916 – March 1921: War Service.
>   September 1921: Marking off, 'Sheads' at Homerton.
>   November 1921: Marking off, Broadwood Whites, Dalston.
>   February 1922: Aeolian Co., Hayes, Middlesex.
>   1922: Commenced evening classes at Northern Poly, Holloway.
>   August 1924: Brasted Bros. Ltd., Harringay (bellying dept.)
>   24th February 1938: founder member of the Institute of Musical Instrument Technology.
>   July 1943: O. Peterson Ltd, Stamford Hill (setting out government contracts).
>   March 1945: Return to Brasteds as 'technical advisor', 7 year agreement.
>   September 23rd 1963: elected Fellow of the Institute of Musical Instrument Technology.
>   August 1970: Retired from Brasteds

12. Patent application 967,321 in the name of Gerald Arthur Brasted, dated 6th October 1959. Complete specification published 19th August 1964. (*Robert Brasted Archive.*)

13. Source of Eavestaff serial numbers and dates: *Pierce Piano Atlas*.

14. Correspondence contained in the John T. Davis Papers, now deposited with Harringay Archives, Bruce Castle Museum, Lordship Lane, London N17 8ND.

15. From the year 2004, pianos bearing the *Eavestaff* name have been manufactured by the Yantai Perzina Piano Manufacturing Company, Yantai, China.

16. Percy Brasted's assertion was recorded in the journal *Musical Opinion*, April 1934.

3. THE SQUIRE FAMILY OF PIANOMAKERS

1. For detailed biographical information about the piano maker John Brinsmead, see: Alastair Laurence, *Five London Piano Makers* pages 13-29.

2. Probate documentation of William Brinsmead Squire of 28, Upper Montague Street, Marylebone, London. Will made 15th March 1862, proved 8th March 1864. (For the text of his will, see appendix 6.)

3. This tale was retold in *The Pianomaker* magazine, March 1914.

4. Details from the London Census Return, 1841.

5. Information about the Devon Youatts and their possible links with the Squire family is available from Bill and Beth Kibby, the Piano History Centre, 271, Southtown Road, Great Yarmouth NR31 0JB.

6. Information also from the Piano History Centre, Great Yarmouth.

7. From the *London Gazette*, issue 22,221, dated the 21st January 1859.

8. From the *London Gazette*, issue 23,569, dated 24th December 1869. Information kindly sourced by Marie Kent (and also information for note 7).

9. The bankruptcy proceedings of Roland M. Squire, Liverpool, 25th August 1873. Information kindly sourced by Helen Weedon.

10. Roland M. Squire of Montreal is recorded as a piano maker still active in the year 1895, when he would have been aged about sixty-two. See: *Pierce Piano Atlas*.

11. Information kindly provided by Frank Squire, great-grandson of Frank Squire of B. Squire & Son.

12. Probate documentation of Frank Squire of 28, Denbigh Road, West Ealing, Middlesex. Will made 15th June 1920, proved 11th June 1923.

13. From *The Pianomaker* magazine, issue April 1923.

14. Information from *The Vale of Bonny in History & Legend* by the Rev. J. Waugh (1982), and *The Bonnybridge Foundries in the Nineteenth Century* by John Ure (1982). Falkirk District Libraries.

15. This only-surviving prices book for Smith & Wellstood cast-iron piano frames (c.1890-c.1915) has been deposited with Falkirk Council Archives, Callendar House, Callendar Park, Falkirk FK1 1YR.

16. Source of information: see note 15 (above).

17. An obituary for John H. Longson appears in *The Pianomaker*, issue March 1916.

18. Byron Squire of Auckland is noted in the book *Piano in the Parlour*, by John MacGibbon, published by Ngaio Press, Wellington, New Zealand (2007). According to his grandson, Donald Squire, Byron would state to his customers that the initial 'B' in *B. Squire & Son* (on the pianos he is likely to have sold in his shop), stood for 'Byron Squire & Son'. This is clearly a piece of misinformation deliberately perpetrated on the unsuspecting New Zealand public!

19. Information from *Lloyds Weekly Newspaper* of the 8th August 1858.

20. Information from the *London Gazette* issue 23,237, 5th April 1867.

21. The *London Gazette*, issue 26,107, dated 18th November 1867, announced that Henry Squire had been discharged from his bankruptcy on the 19th July 1867. Information shown in notes 19, 20 and 21 kindly sourced by Marie Kent.

22. Information received from Frank Squire.

23. From *The Pianomaker* magazine, issue September 1926.

24. From *The Pianomaker* magazine, issue September 1928.

25. The 'bow' drill was the perfect tool for drilling tiny holes in piano bridges to receive the stringing guide pins. It was also used to drill the holes in the wrestplank for tuning pins. The advantages of the bow drill are: a) it is relatively easy to set the precise angle of the bit of the drill, so that the holes in the bridge or wrestplank drilled to receive bridge or tuning pins are angled as accurately as possible; b) there is sensitive control of the speed of the drill bit, simply by increasing or decreasing the speed of movement of the bow with the right arm; c) there is near silence in operation. In contrast, a modem hand-held electric drill is unpleasantly noisy, harder to accurately position for bridge-pin drilling, and the speed of its drill bit can be difficult to control. An electric drill which functions too fast, and which is used with excessive down pressure by the operator, will burn the beech wood from which the bridge is made.

26. Information received from Frank Squire.

4. ROGERS AND HOPKINSON

1. Information kindly provided by John Hopkinson, a descendant of the Hopkinson family of Leeds and London.

2. Information obtained from various Directories of Leeds, early 19th century.

3. In his will dated 23rd March 1886, John Hopkinson of Ynysgain, Criccieth, Carnarvonshire, bequeathed to his nephew James Hopkinson his 'violins and violincelloes'.

4. Wheatley Kirk's design was patented (English patents no.7094). It features the earliest-known design of a complete iron frame for an upright piano. The purpose of the frame was to take the strain of the stringing, whilst at the same time dispensing with the need for the wooden back posts which traditionally strengthen the structure. The removal of the back posts was necessary to make room for Kirk's unique 'double soundboard', which appeared to have had the appearance of a violin (viz: with sides, back, and with sound holes). The patent specification states: *the double sounding board is constructed from the usual wood, but it is enclosed on all sides similar to a violin in the form of a case. It is uniform in its thickness or depth of unoccupied space; it is free and independent of any direct and attached connection with the frame, into which it fits - - - - - The apertures are for the same purpose as what are called sound holes in the violin, namely to give full scope or emission to the tone and its vibration.* (No examples of Kirk's unique piano are known to survive, but a later patented instrument, Dr John Steward's *Euphonicon* (1841), bears a close resemblance in its overall structure to Kirk's earlier design.)

5. Information from the appendix of *A Dictionary of Pianists and Composers for the Pianoforte*, compiled by Ernst Pauer.

6. Quoted in *Musical Instruments in the 1851 Exhibition*, edited by Peter and Ann Mactaggart. Published by Mac & Me Ltd, Welwyn, Herts (1986).

7. Also quoted in note 6.

8. British Patents 3rd December 1851, no. 13,652. Application made in the name of John Hopkinson of Oxford Street in the county of Middlesex, pianoforte manufacturer.

9. An example of a grand piano having Hopkinson's patented action was for many years to be seen at the Leeds College of Music.

10. Patent application October 14th 1872 in the name of Edward Barker Gowland. 'Double bearing on bridge, with down-pressure bar'.

11. Probate documentation for John Hopkinson, who died 4th April 1886. Will made 23rd March 1886, proved 28th May 1886. Value of personal estate: £22,668 8s 5d.

NOTES

12. Information kindly provided by Charles and Caroline Hopkinson.

13. From *The Pianomaker* magazine, issue July 1919.

14. *Five London Piano Makers* by Alastair Laurence. Distributed by Keyword Press. (2010, reprinted 2012).

15. Recorded in *The Pianomaker* magazine, issue February 1924.

16. See note 15 (above).

17. Information received from John Hopkinson.

18. A list of names and addresses of various Rogers individuals making pianos is included in an appendix to *The Pianoforte. Its History Traced to the Great Exhibition of 1851* by Rosamond E. M. Harding. Cambridge University Press (1933).

19. Serial numbers and dates from *Pierce Piano Atlas*.

20. A photograph of the Archer Street factory (Rogers', later Challen's) appears on page 40 of *Five London Piano Makers* (see note 14).

21. *A Treatise on the Art of Pianoforte Construction* published by Unwin Brothers Ltd (1916) and *A Supplement to a Treatise on Pianoforte Construction*, published by King and Jarrett (1927), were both written by Wolfenden.

22. In Samuel Wolfenden's will, made on the 5th March 1929 and proved on the 31st May 1929, some of the bequests made were as follows:

To his cousin Mrs Edith Shackleford: his pianoforte and double music stool and his large aspidistra, and £100.

To Frederic, son of Edith Shackleford: his 'foot lathe standing in my verandah parts of which were at one time the property of his [viz: Frederic's] great grandfather Phillip Skelton Wolfenden and which was rebuilt by me in the year one thousand nine hundred and six'.

To his late wife's 'much loved friend' Mrs Amanda Nicholson: 'the burr walnut tea caddie, work box, stationery cabinet and blotting book made by me as a present to my dear wife'.

To Harry Nicholson: all the books kindly gifted by him to me.

To Walter Pearce: his [the testator's] Starrett micrometer, drawing instruments, scale drafting measures rulers and templates with such other tools 'as he [Walter Pearce] in the discretion of my trustees may select'.

To the Music Trades School at the Northern Polytechnic Holloway Road London N: any articles belonging to him [the testator] 'as may be there at my decease'.

To John Clothier: 'as many of my mounts of microscopic objects as he may select up to one hundred and fifty' and £100.

To Leonard, son of John Clothier: 'my foot lathe now in the loft of my present house with all adjuncts belonging thereto and such other tools as he may desire to be selected by my trustees'.

To Sydney Alfred Hurren: 'such of the remainder of my microscopic objects as he may select up to one hundred'.

23. A letter from Challen and Son to the editor of *The Pianomaker*, issue June 1914, addressed the following important information to the magazine's readership:

We have the honour to inform you that we have concluded arrangements with the Vincent Music Company Ltd whereby we purchase from them, as from this date, all the interests hitherto held by the said company in this business. As a consequence of this transaction, there is no longer any connection between the two firms. Having transferred to the Vincent Music Company (as part of the above mentioned arrangement) the premises hitherto occupied by us in Arlington Road, we have taken a somewhat larger factory situated in Archer Street, Camden Town, to which address we have removed, and where the manufacturing and wholesale departments of the 'Challen' business will henceforth be conducted.

It was noted in *The Pianomaker* magazine, issue October 1920:

W. G. Eavestaff and Sons Ltd: we understand that Messrs George Rogers & Sons (The Vincent Music Co Ltd) have disposed of their interest in the above business to Messrs H.F. & R.A. Brasted, who are now the sole proprietors. (See also chapter 2 of this book, dealing with the Eavestaff and Brasted firms).

24. Piano numbers and dates from *Pierce Piano Atlas*.

25. Information obtained from a Rogers publicity brochure, c.1938. *(Author's collection.)*

26. From *The Pianomaker*, issue January 1926.

27. Price list of Rogers pianos, c.1938. *(Author's collection.)*

28. A careful examination of photographs in the archives of Booth & Brookes Ltd, ironfounders of Burnham-on-Crouch, Essex, shows that upright piano frames made for the Orchestrelle Company of Hayes, Middlesex, in the 1920s, appear to be identical to iron frames made during the 1930s for George Rogers & Sons. (*Essex County Record Office, Chelmsford. CM2 6YT*.)

29. Information kindly provided by Allan Lanstein.

5. ALFRED KNIGHT

1. The London Census Return of 1901 shows the Knight family to be living at 15, Lornwood Road, Newington, Southwark, south London. In the Census, twenty-five-year-old Alfred Knight senior's occupation is shown as being that of a 'Regulating contractor, pianofortes'.

2. Information from a huge scrapbook of family and business information, initially compiled by Alfred Knight, and then after Knight's death continued by his daughter and son-in-law, Sylvia and John York. A great deal of material for this chapter has been sourced from this same scrapbook.

3. These particular *Squire & Longson* frame designs are shown in the photographic records of the ironfounders, Booth & Brookes Ltd, of Burnham-on-Crouch, Essex. *Essex County Record Office, Chelmsford*. The 'girder' frame for the upright model C26 is illustrated on page 99 of the publication, *Five London Piano Makers*, by Alastair Laurence.

4. Information kindly provided by Sylvia York.

5. John Forrester Ltd (incorporated in the year 1912) was compulsorily wound up on the 13th October 1931 on the petition of E. Quitman Ltd. Creditors were owed £588, of which Quitman was owed £50. Source of information: *The Pianomaker* magazine, issue October 1931.

6. The first Booker/Knight iron-frame casting of the re-modelled Forrester upright appears in a photograph from Booth & Brookes' archives. The photograph is dated the 22nd July 1932. (See also the photograph on page 84).

7. The rim-bending press for the six-foot Marshall & Rose grand is now in the possession of John Broadwood & Sons Ltd (2015).

8. Information from Sylvia York.

9. The dates and serial numbers, from which estimated annual Knight production has been determined, have been obtained from *Pierce Piano Atlas*.

10. Monington & Weston's 'double iron frame' system of piano construction was known as the *Tuplex*, and was designed by William Shepherd Watts (1885-1974), the owner of the company. Although the patent was applied for on the 24th December 1925, the system was not actually used in piano production until 1932. The 'Tuplex' was incorporated into five designs of upright piano and two designs of baby grand. Pianos incorporating the 'Tuplex' feature continued to be manufactured by Monington & Weston until that firm closed down in 1976. Source of information: Bernard Watts.

11. See: *The Broadwood Barless Piano. A History*, by Alastair Laurence. First published in 2004. Twice reprinted, with corrections, 2011 and 2014.

12. Michael Cockram was a piano dealer in The Headrow, Leeds, Yorkshire, whose firm, *R. Barker and Company*, was a Knight stockist.

13. Information from the Knight scrapbook. See note 2.

14. Information from the booklet, *The Ironfoundry at Burnham*, written by John Booth, a former director of Booth & Brookes.

15. These statistics have been obtained by analysing serial numbers and dates in *Pierce Piano Atlas*.

16. Information from *The Essex Countryside Magazine*, issue August 1966.

17. Information from the *Gazette & Guardian*, November 1967.

18. Quoted in *The International Businessman's Who's Who*, 2nd edition (undated, 1960s).

19. From an obituary written by Bernard Comsky, which appeared in the November 1974 issue of *The Journal of the American Piano Tuners' Guild*.

20. The disastrous collapse of the educational piano market also seriously affected the London firm of W. Danemann and Company, who specialised in the production of school instruments. The factory of the Danemann company closed down in 1984. See: *Five London Piano Makers*, chapter 4.

APPENDIX 1
A list of employees of the Chappell Piano Company who lost their lives in World War I.

J. T. Abrams	G. W. Cotton	T. E. Misson
E. A. Adams	J. F. Cos	H. Mockridge
J. A. C. Adcock	W. J. Cos	T. B. Nunn
E. N. Baillie	A. E. Ellis	H. J. O'Day
W. A. G. Benson	F. A. Finch	W. C. Page
A. C. Board	G. Flint	R. W. Pearce
A. V. Brandon	W. E. French	W. S. Pevier
E. L. Bridges	W. J. Kirk	H. E. F. Schulz
R. C. Casey	A. G. Lane	A. Ward
H. Cole	R. H. Langley	C. A. Warwick
J. R. Collins	A. Mayhew	J. Webb
W. Cook	A. J. Meadows	F. J. Williams
S. A. Cooper	H. F. Meekings	

These names appear on a 'Roll of Honour' plaque which was affixed to the wall of the factory premises in the yard to the rear of the main (Belmont Street) building.
(2014: the plaque is now attached to a wrought-iron gate which is presently free-standing in the yard.)

APPENDIX 2
Chappell Retail Price List, October 1929

GRANDS	Guineas
Concert grand	507
Boudoir grand (3 legs)	330
Mignon grand (3 legs)	260
New Bijou 5' 3" grand (6 legs)	189
New 'Pearl' grand (3 legs)	144
Grands fitted with 6 legs (extra)	6

UPRIGHTS	
Model 'Diamond'	111
Model 'Emerald'	100
Model 'Emerald Jacobean'	96
Model 'Ruby'	90
Model 'Student'	77

PLAYER PIANOS	
Mignon Grand Player (Higel Metal Action)	507
New Bijou 5' 3" Player (Higel Metal Action)	72
'Diamond' Player (Higel Metal Action)	213
'Diamond' Player (Higel Wood Action)	186
'E' Player	154

Source: from the late Perry Cossins Papers, Scunthope.

Rogers Retail Price List, circa 1938

GRANDS	Guineas
Drawing Room, 6' 8"	217
Boudoir, 6' 0"	194
Baby, 5' 0"	141
Junior, 6 legs, 4' 6"	123
Junior, 3 legs, 4' 6"	117
Miniature, 4' 3"	93

UPRIGHTS	
Model 6	99
Model 1 'Jacobean'	88
Model 1 'Vocalist'	88
Model 0	78
Model 56	66

PLAYER PIANOS	
Grand player, 5' 1"	229
Upright Player de Luxe	135
Upright Player	117

Source: price list in the Author's Collection

APPENDIX 3
An outline tree of the Brasted family of piano makers

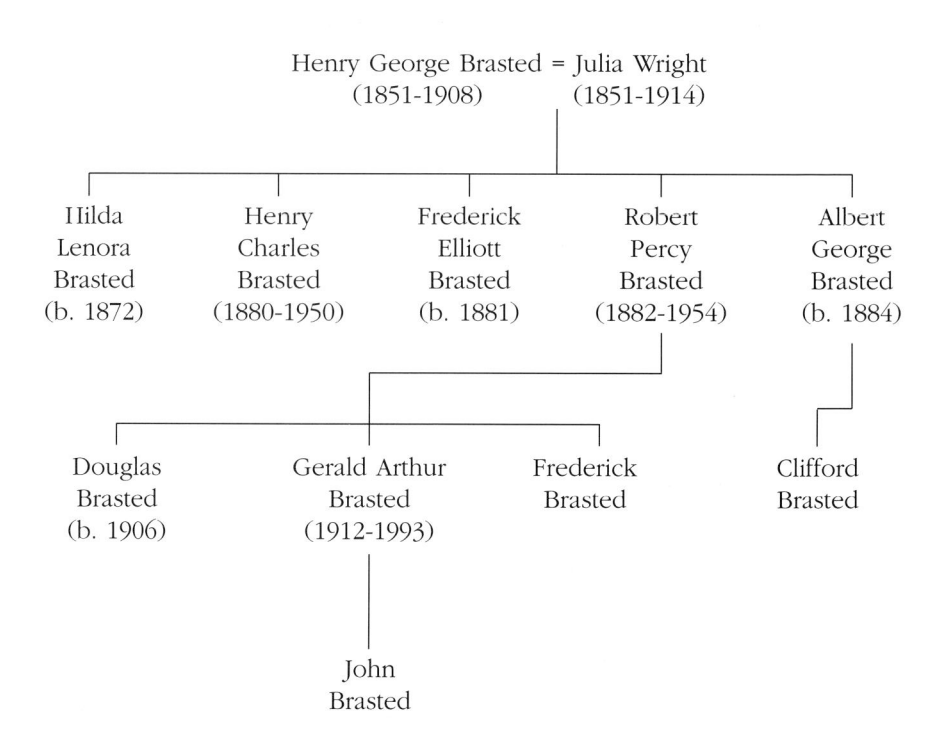

```
              Henry George Brasted = Julia Wright
                   (1851-1908)        (1851-1914)
```

- Hilda Lenora Brasted (b. 1872)
- Henry Charles Brasted (1880-1950)
- Frederick Elliott Brasted (b. 1881)
- Robert Percy Brasted (1882-1954)
- Albert George Brasted (b. 1884)

Children of Robert Percy Brasted:
- Douglas Brasted (b. 1906)
- Gerald Arthur Brasted (1912-1993)
- Frederick Brasted

Child of Albert George Brasted:
- Clifford Brasted

Child of Gerald Arthur Brasted:
- John Brasted

APPENDIX 4

Checklist of new models of upright, grand and minipiano introduced by Brasted Brothers Ltd, between the years 1930 and 1969:

1930: 'Hayes' model upright (from Aeolian Company).
1931: 4' 6" baby grand, designed by Mr Longhurst of Challen.
1934: Six-octave *rear action* minipiano (from Lundholm).
1935: 4' 3" baby grand, designed by Jack Davis.
1936: Six-octave *front action* minipiano, designed by Jack Davis.
1937: 'Minigrand' upright piano, model 604, designed by Jack Davis.
1938: Seven-octave minipiano, model 7FA (from Nyland, Sweden).
1938: Seven-octave 'Miniroyal', model 801, with broken hammer line (from Schimmel).
1939: 4' 0" upright, model 701, designed by Jack Davis.
1940: Seven octave minipiano, model MP85 with longer bass strings, designed by Jack Davis.
1940: Seven-and-one-quarter octave minipiano, MP88, a development of the previous model, designed by Jack Davis.
1948: 4' 8" baby grand, model 900, designed by Jack Davis.
1958: 'Miniroyal' model 90, with improved long bass strings and inclined hammer line, internally designed by Jack Davis. (Case design by Mr Hadden.)
1962: 'Challen' upright, model 988, designed by Jack Davis.
1967-68: 'Minitronic' electro-acoustic keyboard. Stringing design by Pasquali.
1969: 3' 4" upright, model 585, designed by Jack Davis.

Source: the Jack Davis Papers

APPENDIX 5

An outline tree of the Squire family of piano makers

The numbers shown against each name refer to the numbers used in the chapter in the book dealing with the Squire family.

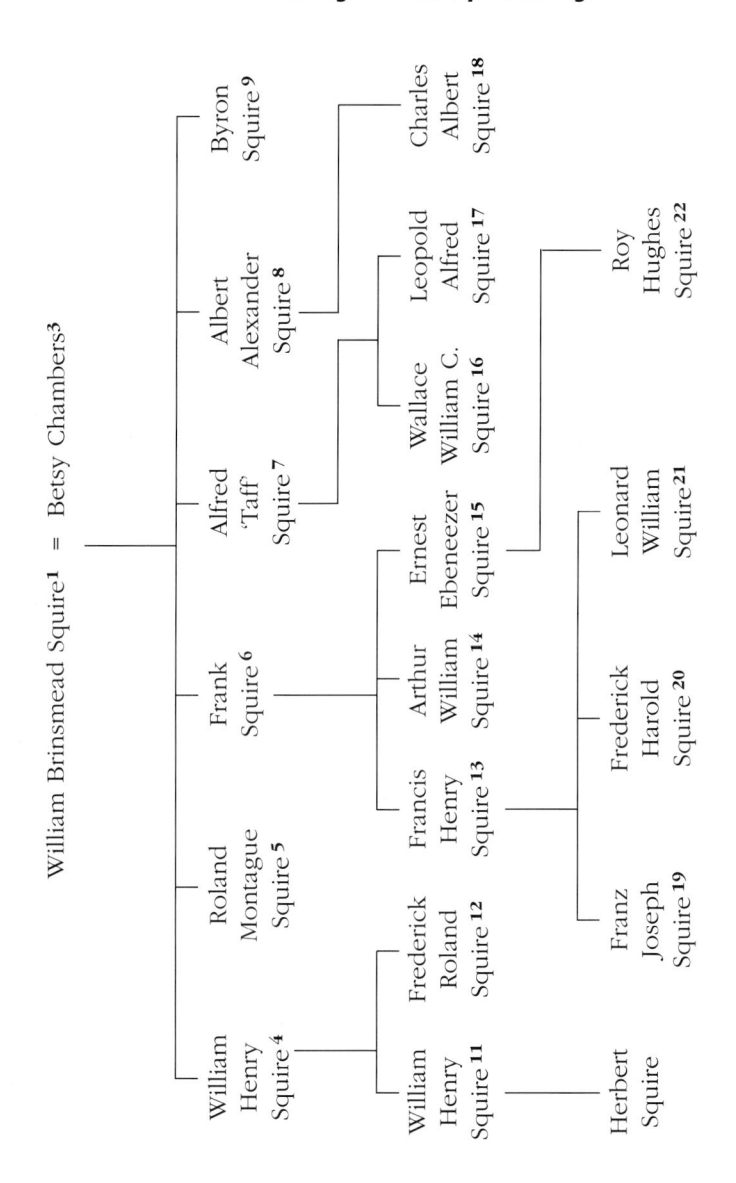

William Brinsmead Squire[1] = Betsy Chambers[3]

- William Henry Squire[4]
  - Frederick Roland Squire[12]
- Roland Montague Squire[5]
  - William Henry Squire[11]
  - Francis Henry Squire[13]
    - Franz Joseph Squire[19]
    - Herbert Squire
- Frank Squire[6]
  - Arthur William Squire[14]
    - Frederick Harold Squire[20]
    - Leonard William Squire[21]
  - Ernest Ebeneezer Squire[15]
- Alfred 'Taff' Squire[7]
- Albert Alexander Squire[8]
  - Wallace William C. Squire[16]
    - Roy Hughes Squire[22]
  - Leopold Alfred Squire[17]
  - Charles Albert Squire[18]
- Byron Squire[9]

APPENDIX 6

The last will of William Brinsmead Squire, who died on the 25th January 1864. Will made 15th March 1862; proved 8th March 1864.

The Last Will and Testament of **William Brinsmead Squire**, of 28, Upper Montague Street in the Parish of St Marylebone London Pianoforte Manufacturer made this fifteenth day of March one thousand eight hundred and sixty two.

I give and bequeath unto my well beloved wife Betsy all my property of every kind whatsoever for her sole use and benefit during her life. I likewise will and desire that my business of a Pianoforte Manufacturer should be carried on by my Executors for the bringing up and educating of my children who are minors.

And I also wish that my son Frank who has conducted my business under my instruction and to my satisfaction should continue so to conduct the same under the orders and control of my Executors at a fair remunerative salary.

I will also that at the death of my beloved wife Betsy all property of every kind whatsoever (saving and excepted that which is hereafter named) as soon as my Executors or their assigns may seem fit be sold and an equal division to be made among my then surviving children.

My son Roland Montague Squire now of Liverpool being indebted to me the sum of three hundred pounds I will that the same be payable on the demand of my Executors and to bear interest from this date at the rate of four per cent per annum.

My son William is also indebted to me in the sum of thirty pounds. I will that it be payable in the same manner as the aforesaid.

My son Frank is likewise indebted to me in the sum of twenty pounds. I will that it be payable in the same manner as the aforesaid. I will that should those several sums in which my sons may be indebted to my estate not be paid off at the death of my wife then my surviving trustee or his assigns shall in the division of property among my children charge those debts and interests severally due from those my sons or their assigns to them as a set off against the claim they may have to their share of my property.

I will also that as a reward to my son Frank for the fidelity with which I believe he will carry on this my business for his mother and the younger branches of the family that at the death of my beloved wife my trustee or his assigns do give to him the business of a Pianoforte Manufacturer together with the following articles applicable to the said trade viz. Benches Iron Pots and Wood Clamps Wood and Metal Cauls Patterns Scales Moulds German Stoves or steam apparatus but not to include boiler engine or machinery of steam power foot lathes all gas fittings and its appurtenances in the shop.

In order to carry out these my wishes and requests I do hereby appoint my beloved wife and Mr George Speechly of 56, Aldersgate Street in the City of London my executors to carry out the same. As witnessed my hand this fifteenth day of March in the Year of Our Lord One thousand eight hundred and sixty two [signed] **W.B. Squire**. Signed and witnessed in the presence of the testator and in the presence of each other. Wm Robertson Senr. Wm Robertson Junr.

(From the Principal Probate Registry)

APPENDIX 7
An outline tree of the Hopkinson family of piano makers

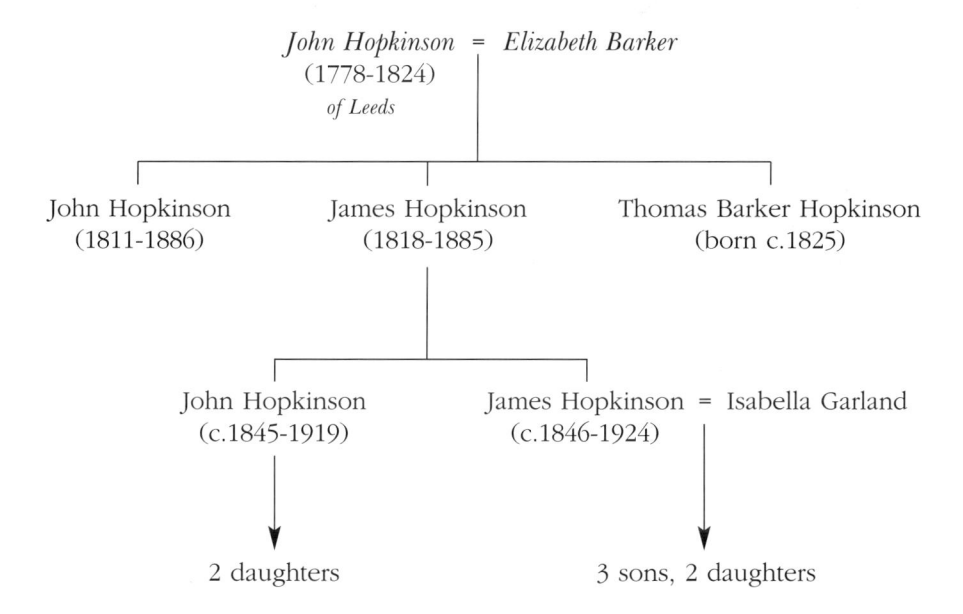

```
                John Hopkinson  =  Elizabeth Barker
                  (1778-1824)
                    of Leeds
      ┌──────────────────┼──────────────────────────┐
John Hopkinson      James Hopkinson       Thomas Barker Hopkinson
 (1811-1886)          (1818-1885)              (born c.1825)
                 ┌─────────┴──────────┐
          John Hopkinson        James Hopkinson  =  Isabella Garland
          (c.1845-1919)          (c.1846-1924)
                ↓                       ↓
           2 daughters            3 sons, 2 daughters
```

APPENDIX 8
A selection of favourable testimonials which had been received by the firm of George Rogers & Sons by circa 1933

Vladimir de Pachmann (1848-1933), concert pianist: *I have been much delighted with the perfect responsiveness and charm of tone of the Rogers Pianos. They are without doubt the foremost British Pianos of the present day.*

Stewart Macpherson (1865-1941), professor, Royal Academy of Music: *I have the greatest pleasure in stating that the Rogers Upright which I have in constant use completely satisfies all my requirements. It is a really artistic instrument which would be hard to beat.*

Sir Henry J. Wood (1869-1944), conductor: *I have lately acquired one of the new model small Grands, and I must say that it gives me the utmost pleasure to make music upon it. Perfection of touch, beautiful quality of tone and warm resonance are there, and only need sympathetic treatment to fascinate any and all kinds of listeners.*

Dr Percy C. Buck (1871-1947), musical director, Harrow School: *I have tried the Rogers Pianos at Harrow with entirely satisfactory results. Used by all sorts and conditions of boys, they obviously have to stand an unusual strain, and I can guarantee that they have survived the ordeal as well as any piano I have ever tried.*

Percy A. Scholes (1877-1958), music critic and journalist: *I have sold my German Piano and bought a British one. I have chosen a Rogers. There are other good British makes, but the Rogers Piano appeals to me particularly. Its tone and its touch are everything I could wish, and not one of my musical friends who has tried it can make any adverse criticism on any point; but then, I find they mostly have Rogers too, or if they have not, are only waiting an opportunity to sell their German piano and get a Rogers.* [The jingoism surrounding this testimonial suggests that it is likely to have been received during the First World War period.]

Joseph Holbrooke (1878-1958), composer: *I must congratulate you on your fine piano. After a good trial I must particularly mention your light and charming touch.*

Sir Thomas Beecham (1879-1961), conductor: *I have been using a Rogers Upright Piano and I have found it ideally suited to my work. The tone is delicate, sympathetic, and entirely devoid of the harshness too often associated with a small piano.*

Mark Hambourg (1879-1960), concert pianist: *I have known the Rogers Pianos for many years, but your new models are far in advance of previous experience. Their tonal qualities and remarkably responsive touch are a delight to the musician, and I can most thoroughly recommend them to all who require a really good musical instrument, and one which will last a lifetime.*

C. Armstrong Gibbs (1889-1960), composer: *I can conscientiously say that it is the finest upright I have ever played on.*

Source of information:
a Rogers publicity brochure of early 1930s date, Author's Collection.

APPENDIX 9

Reminiscences of George Veness, a keyboard technician and music stand maker, (born 1947) who was working at the Rogers/Hopkinson factory, Paxton Road, Tottenham, north London, during the early 1970s.

Herbert Lowrey ran the workplace. Very much hands-on, he was involved in the fine tuning and checking over. We made the upright Rogers 7 octave. Occasionally a *Steinberg* version, which was much the same. We were known in the trade for making 'Zender's posh stuff'. About fifteen workers. I was employed as a 'marker off' – drilling the tuning pin holes in the plank, carving the bridge, fitting bridge pins. This was very labour intensive. I recall making a bridge-pin punch using rat-tail files and a screw driver end from a brace-and-bit, so that the [marking out for] three tri-cord holes could be punched all at once.

Next to us were the two 'go-bar decks': the presses for glueing the ribs and rims to the soundboards, the tables of which I think were made slightly concave [to aid creation of soundboard curvature]. Next to us the stringer's wire was housed in wooden boxes on the wall. Roslau plated wire was used – except for the top octave or so, where polished wire was preferred. I worked under an experienced craftsman well over pensionable age, and a colleague. Pay was delivered in cash weekly: the two men compared notes saying 'six' or 'five' depending on how many £5 notes they received! Once a week, Fletcher & Newman's rep. came round [selling tools and materials].

When ready, the piano backs were moved into the adjoining case fitters' room [for the next stage of construction] – a father and son team who ran a carpentry business fitting wardrobes at the weekends.

About twice a year the factory took delivery of a batch of baby grands by Sojin. The workforce had to tune, regulate and touch up where required, and then send them off to Harrods. The instruments arrived in cases made of solid mahogany type redwood, very desirable timber which was then appropriated by the case fitters for their weekend work!

Sometimes at the end of the day Mr Lowrey would perform on one of his finished uprights: usually a Mendelssohn *Song Without Words*. He was a fine pianist. I learned later that he invigilated at the student piano tuners' Passing Out Exams at the London College of Furniture.

(Note: as the Paxton Road factory had no machine shop, it is likely that all the necessary wooden components were machined in the Zender factory at Hackney.)

APPENDIX 10
Key Knight personnel involved in piano manufacture, c.1950–1990

Granville Park Works, Edmonton:

Jack Knight: back and soundboard foreman, cousin of Alfred Knight.
Harry Knight: factory manager, also cousin of Alfred Knight.
Bill Jamison: polishing foreman.
Harry Ansell: action regulating foreman.
Harry Demonte: head tuner and toner.

Loughton Factory:

Norman Bell: marking off.
Bernard Brewer: mill manager and production officer from 1954.
Tom Chubb: action regulation foreman.
Harry Cowland: mill foreman from 1970.
Bill Drew: staining, filling and polishing.
Jimmy Ellis: bellying (soundboards).
Jack Gooch: fly-finishing foreman from 1954.
Robert Jennings: pattern maker and tool jig maker, maintenance engineer of all plant and machines.
Tony Norgate: polishing foreman from 1960.
Allan Townsend: veneer foreman from 1975.

Michael York: senior manager of production, Alfred Knight's grandson.
Sylvia and John York: directors, daughter and son-in-law of Alfred Knight.

Source of information: Sylvia and Michael York.

APPENDIX 11

May 1969: Lowest prices for various English upright models of seven or seven-and-one-quarter octave compass

Chappell	'model B'	£323	0	0	
Danemann	'slim 85'	320	5	0	
Challen	'988'	316	0	0	
Collard	'8c'	316	0	0	(made by Chappell)
Broadwood	'65'	305	0	0	(made by Kemble)
Welmar	'41'	299	0	0	
Knight	'K6'	291	0	0	
Monington/Weston	'Consort'	275	0	0	
Rogers	'106'	275	0	0	
Kemble	'Minuet'	266	0	0	
Brinsmead	'Regency'	263	0	0	(made by Kemble)
Eavestaff	'585'	244	0	0	(made by Brasted)
Zender	'Royalette'	231	5	0	
Bentley	'Compact 85'	214	0	0	
Giles	'Blenheim'	210	0	0	
(Compared with):					
Steinway	'Model F'	£684	0	0	
Blüthner		660	0	0	

Six-octave models:

Kemble	'Minor'	£225	0	0
Zender	'Strathmore'	215	0	0
Giles	'Arundel'	210	0	0
Bentley	'Compact 73'	199	0	0

Source: The Jack Davis Papers

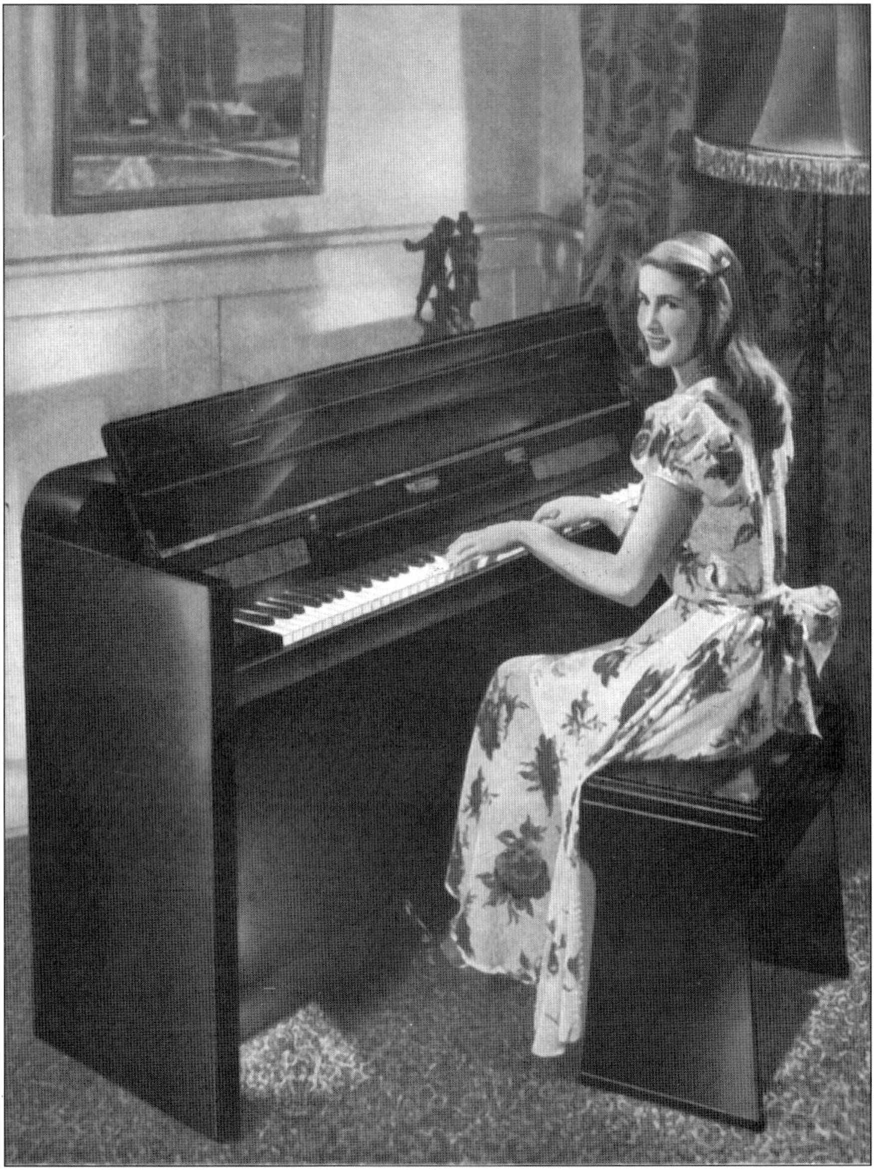